E S T A T E   P U B L I C A T I O N S

LONDON BOROUGH OF **BROM**

G000113855

	Eltham **4** Mottingha				

Penge **6** Beckenham **7**	**8** BROMLEY **9**	**10** Chislehurst **11** Bickley	**12** St. Paul's Cray **13** Foots Cray
Eden Park **14** Addiscombe **15**	**16** Hayes **17** West Wickham	**18** Petts Wood **19** Orpington	**20** St. Mary Cray **21**
	22 New Addington **23**	**24** Farnborough **25** Pratt's Bottom	**26** Chelsfield **27**
	28 Leaves Green **29** Downe	**30** Cudham **31**	
	32 Biggin Hill **33** Tatsfield	**34**	

ROAD MAP pages 2 - 3
INDEX TO STREETS page 37

Every effort has been made to verify the accuracy of information in this book but the publishers cannot accept responsibility for expense or loss caused by an error or omission. Information that will be of assistance to the user of the maps will be welcomed.

The representation on these maps of a road, track or path is no evidence of the existence of a right of way.

Car Park	P
Public Convenience	C
Place of Worship	+
One-way Street	→
Pedestrianized	
Post Office	●

**Scale of street plans 4 inches to 1 mile
Unless otherwise stated**

Street plans prepared and published by ESTATE PUBLICATIONS, Bridewell House, TENTERDEN, KENT.
The Publishers acknowledge the co-operation of the local authorities
of towns represented in this atlas.

Ordnance Survey® This product includes mapping data licensed from Ordnance Survey®
with the permission of the Controller of Her Majesty's Stationery Office.

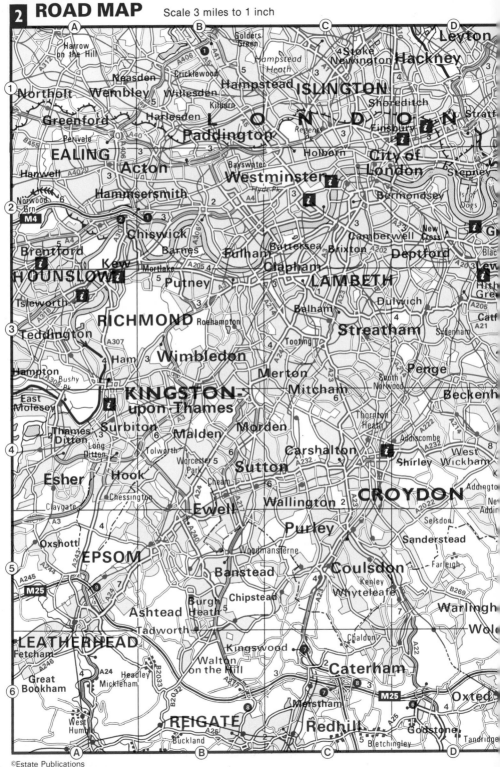

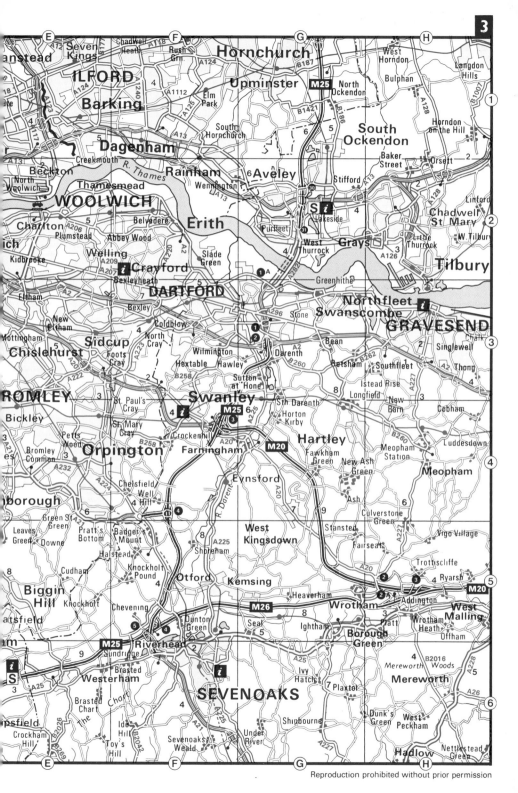

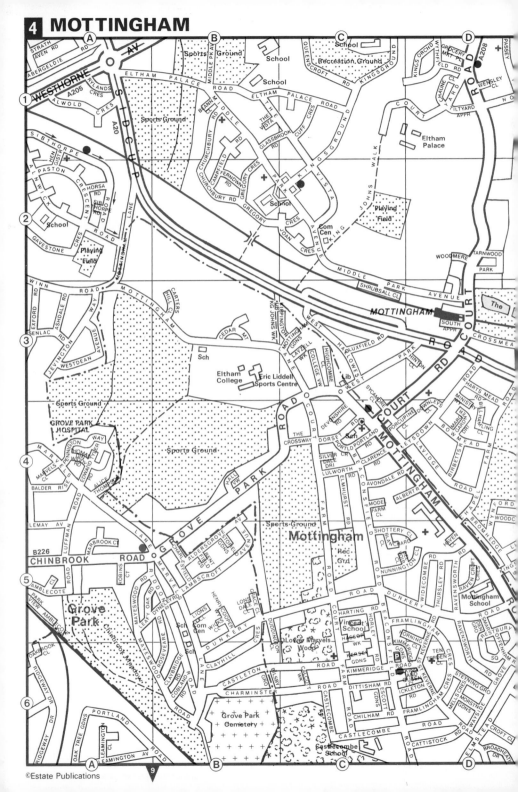

NEW ELTHAM 5

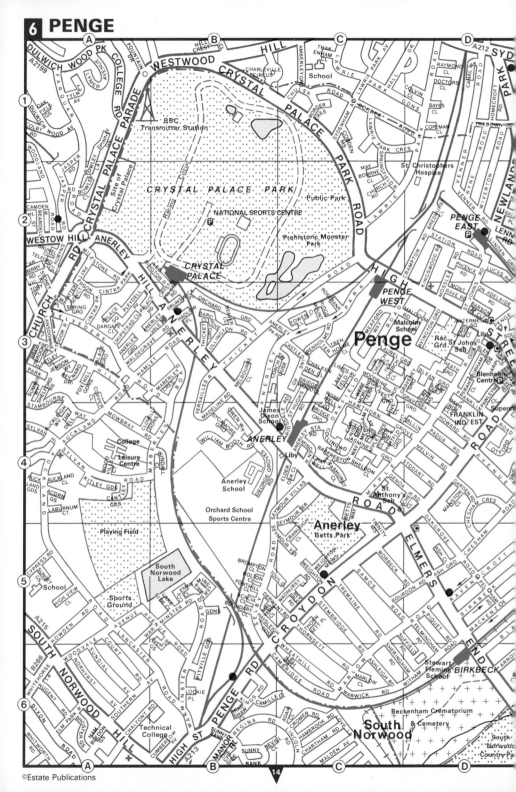

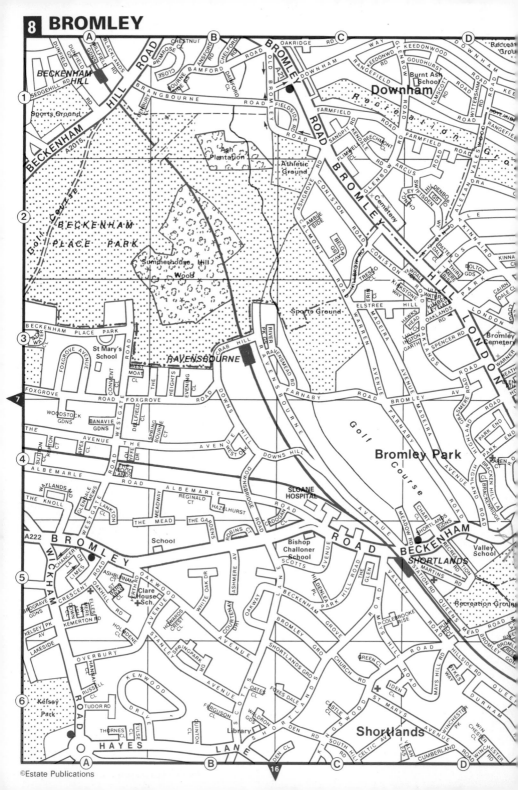

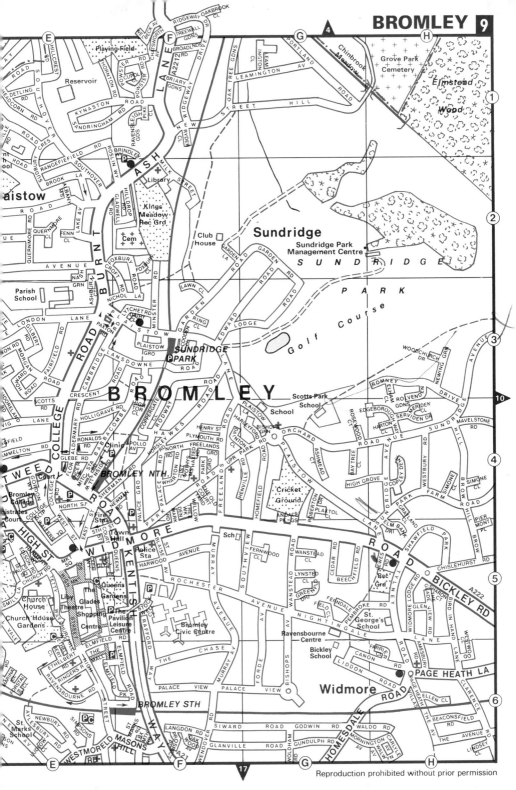

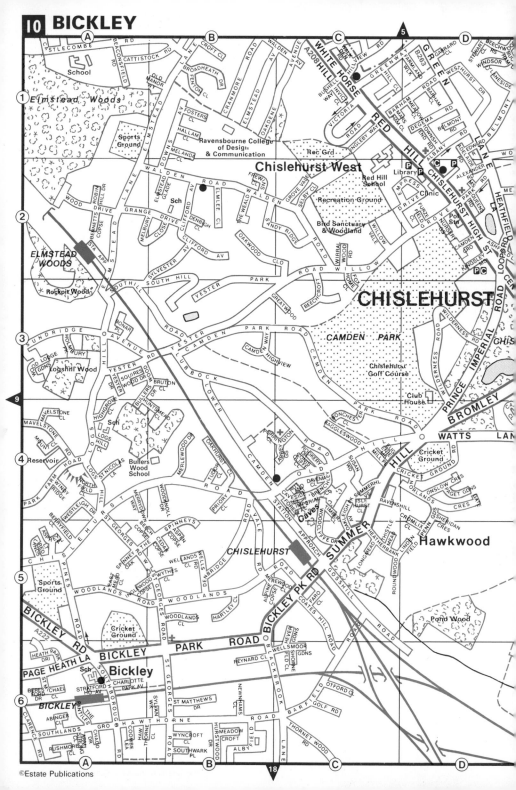

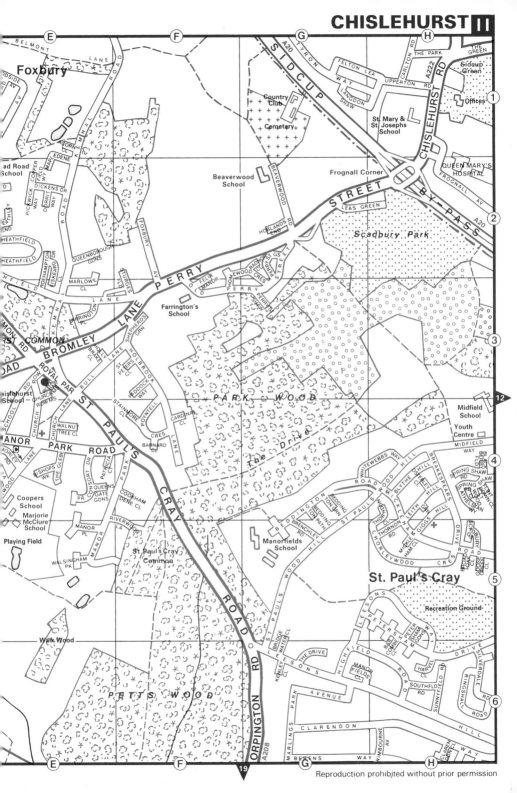

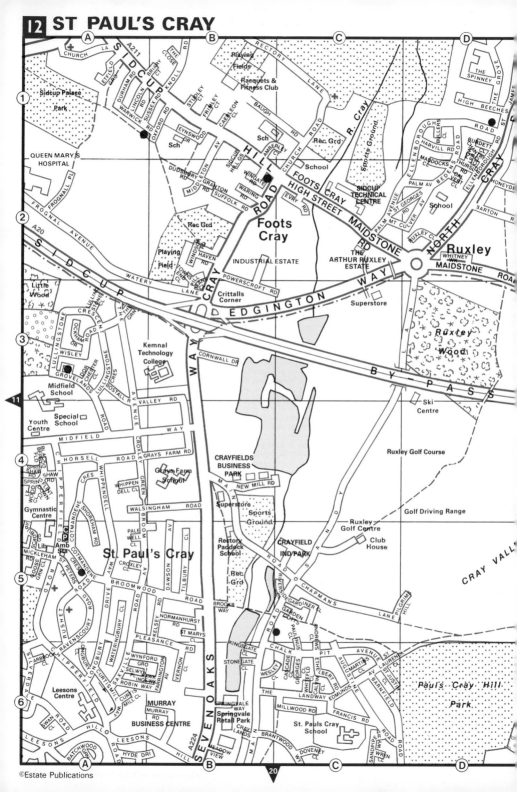

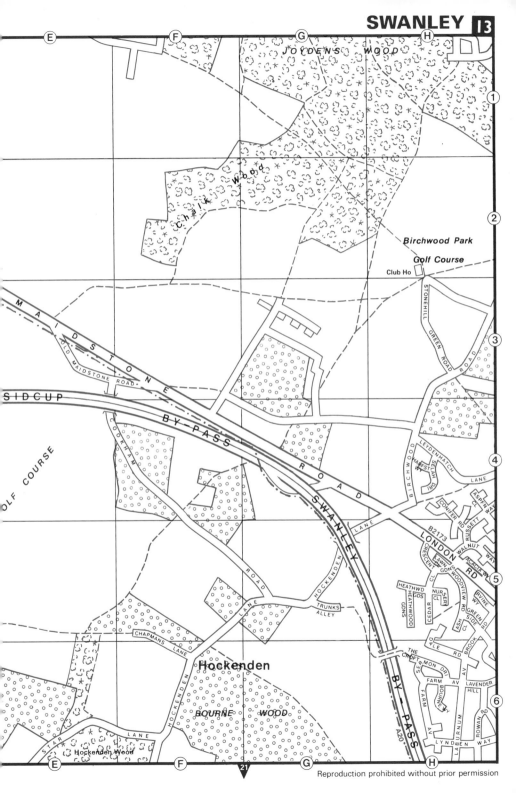

JOYDEN'S WOOD

Chalk Wood

Birchwood Park
Golf Course
Club Ho

STONEHILL GREEN ROAD

MAIDSTONE

OLD MAIDSTONE ROAD

SIDCUP

BY-PASS ROAD

SWANLEY

GOLF COURSE

OLF COURSE

COOKHAM

BIRCHWOOD ROAD

LEYDENHATCH LANE

WARFST WY

LELAND RD

LANE

CONIFER CL

ROSSETT CL

ASPEN WAY

B2173

LONDON RD

CRESCENT RD

LAWN GDNS

WOODVIEW RD

WALNUT WY

ACACIA W

IRVINE WY

GREEN CL

ROW

HOCKENDEN LANE

TRUNKS ALLEY

HEATHWD GDNS

HEATHWOOD GDNS

NURSERY CL

CEDAR RD

ASH RD

ROADSIDE

CHAPMANS LANE

HOCKENDEN LANE

LANE

ROAD

Hockenden

THE CROFT

MON DRI

OYLE RD

BROOK

FARM AV

BOURNE WY

LAVENDER HILL

BY-PASS

A20

BOURNE WOOD

STAR LANE

Hockenden Wood

LABURNUM AV

LYNDHURST AV

ROWAN RD

GREEN WAY

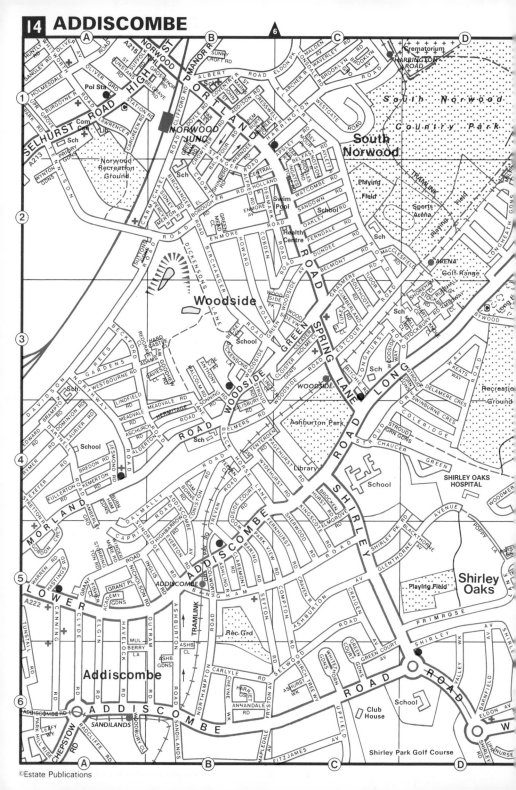

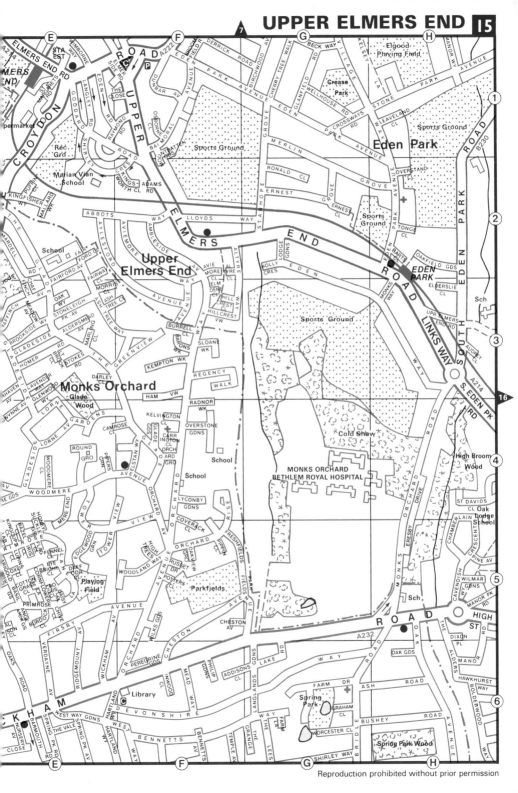

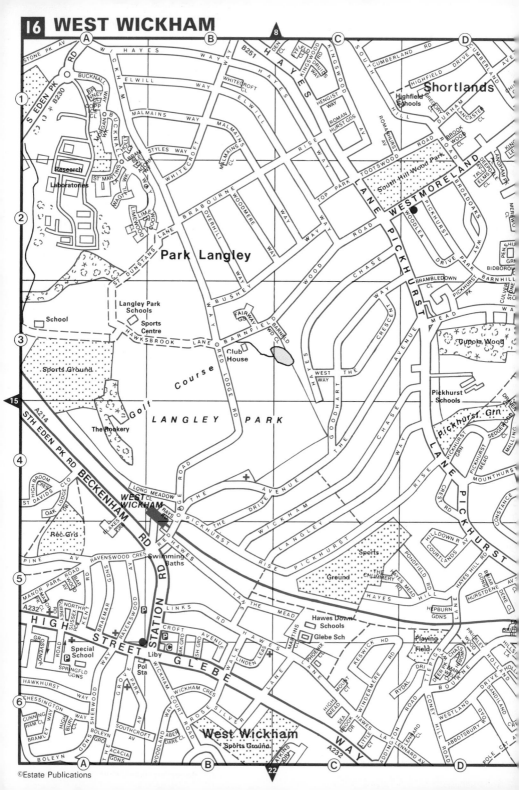

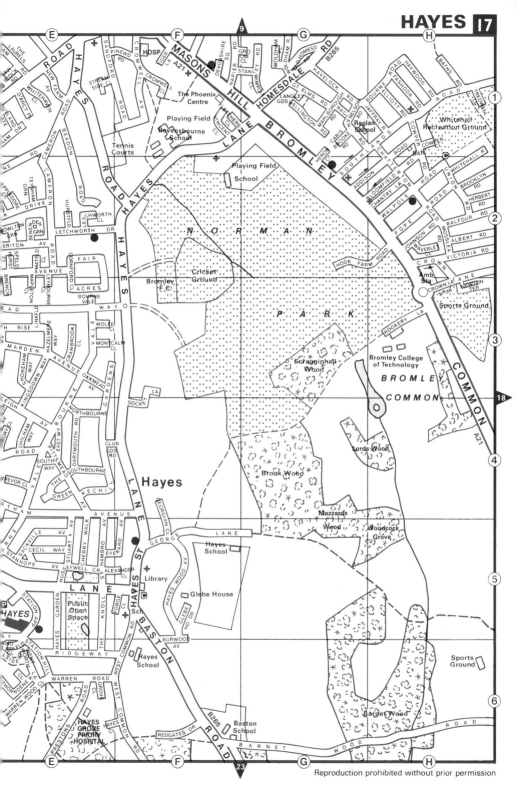

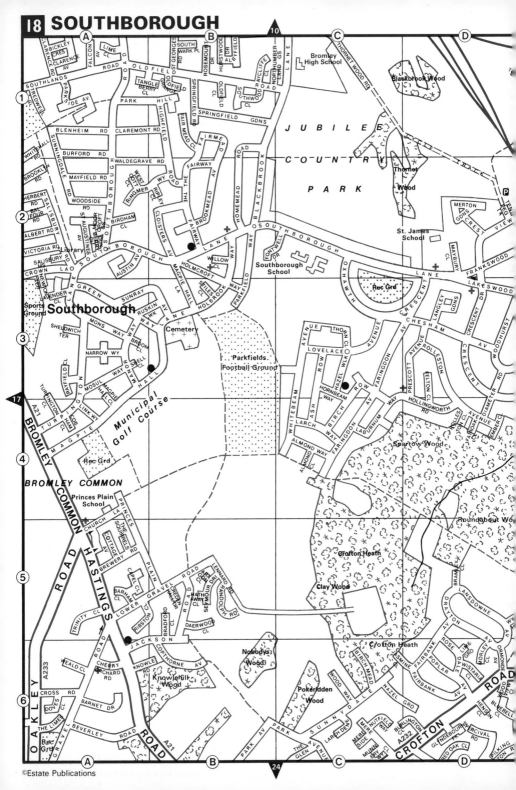

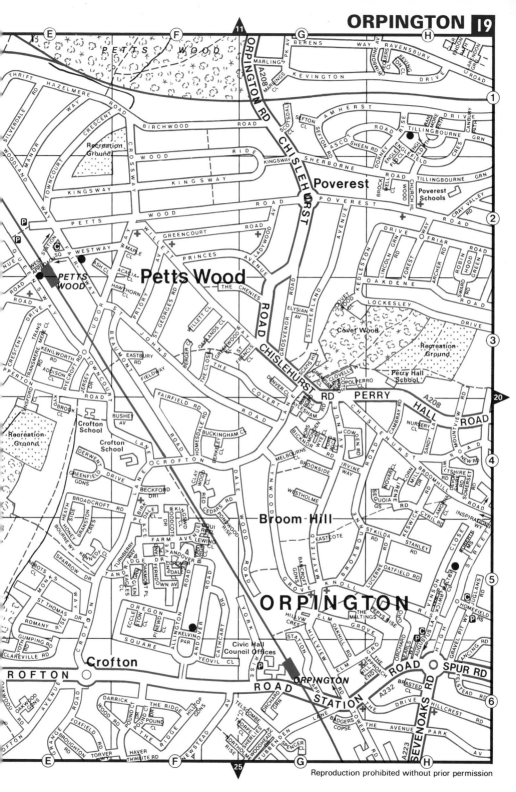

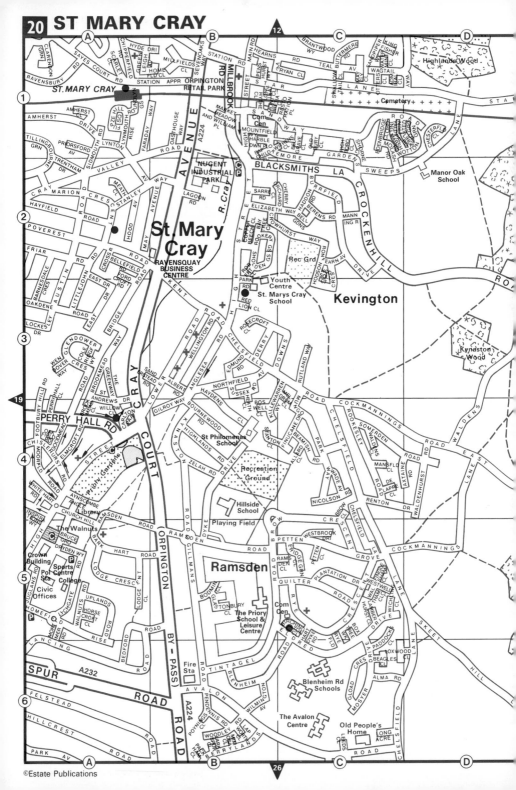

Hockenden Wood

BOURNE WOOD

SWANLEY BY-PASS

A20

Brick Works

STONES CROSS

GREENCOURT RD

ROAD

Rec Grd

SHEEPCOTE

CROCKENHILL

STONES CROSS ROAD

THE GREEN

Sch

GRN COURT RD

B258

SEVEN ACRES

ROAD

BROADWAY

BRANSELL CL

Crockenhill

WEST VW

RD

MAIN RD

ROAD

CRAY

ROAD

SOUNDS LODGE

TYLERS GREEN

CHAPEL RD

OLD CHAPEL RD

TUDOR CT

CHURCH FARM CL

CHURCH ROAD

BARNFIELD CL

NEWPORTS

HARVEST WAY

ROAD

WOODMAN

Wood

GORSE LANE

ROAD

DALTONS ROAD

DALTONS ROAD

IBBS

KEET

HILL LANE

ROAD

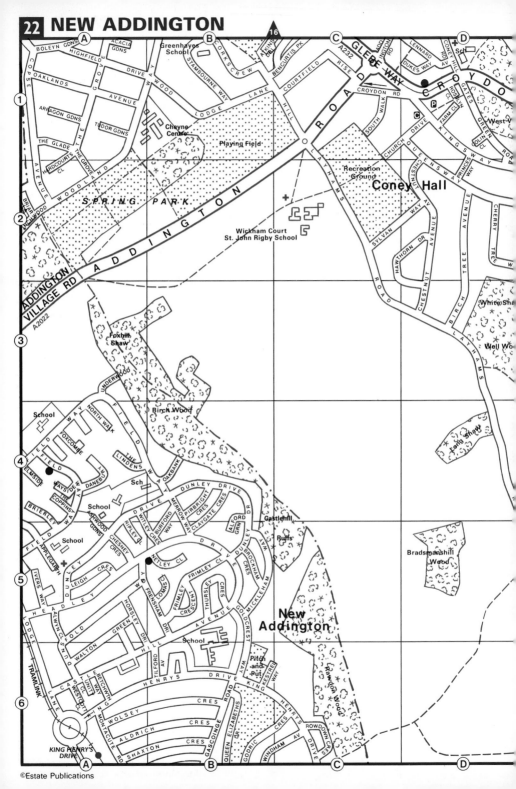

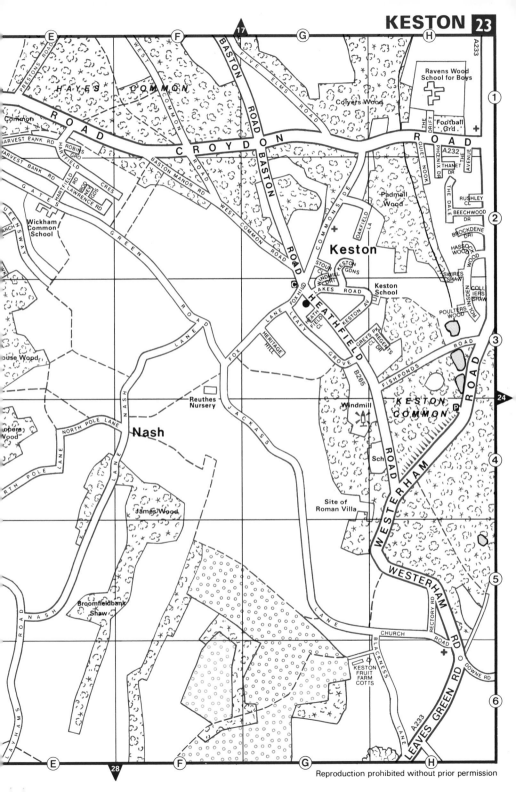

Keston Mark

Locksbottom

Farnborough

South Park

CÆSARS CAMP

Holwood

Ninhams Wood

Farnborough Reservoir

The Larches

Darrick Wood Schools

Sports Centre

Farnborough Hospital

Farnborough School

Farthing Street

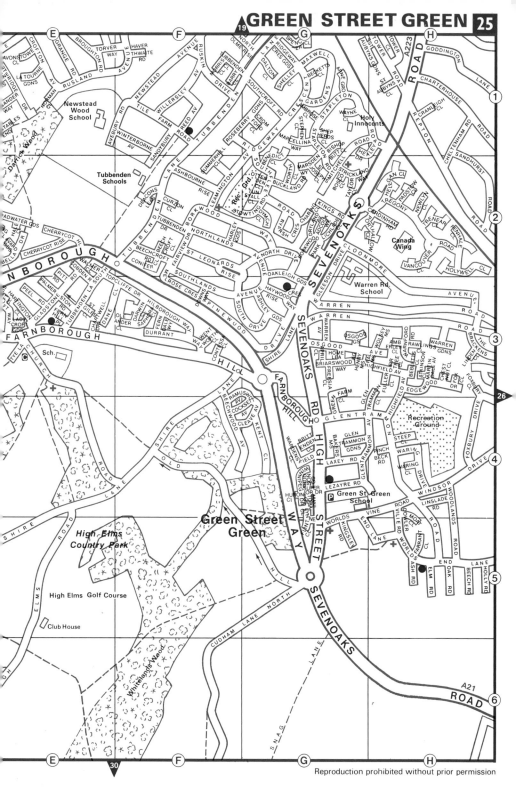

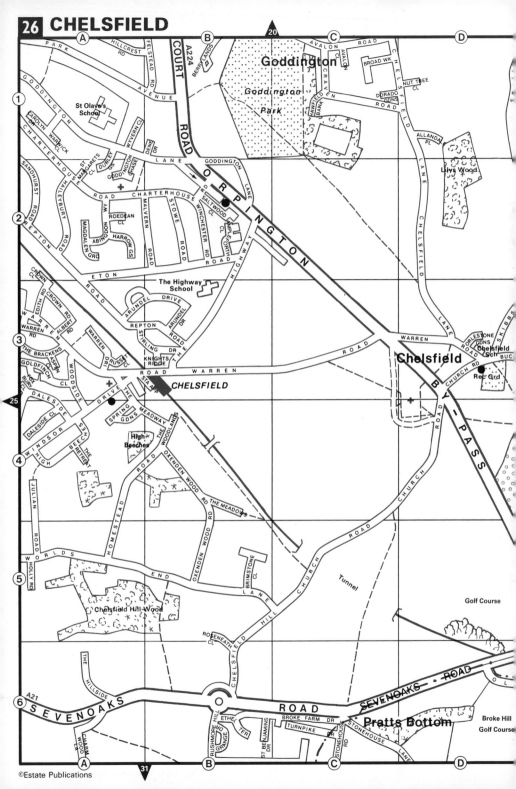

21

E F G H

1
2
3
4
5
6

Crown Wood
GORSE RD
SKEET HILL LANE
COOKHAM HILL
Playing Field
DALTONS ROAD
Skeet Hill
SKEET HILL LANE
PARKGATE
ROAD
M25
Black Bush Wood
Owen Wood
WELL HILL
FIRMINGERS
CHELSFIELD PARK HOSPITAL
HAWSTEAD
School
PUMP LANE
ROAD
OSS
MAYPOLE
JUBILEE
ROCK ROAD
PUMP HILL
WELL HILL
ROCK HILL
REDMANS LANE
Maypole
ROAD
HOLLYBUSH LA
SHOREHAM LANE
Reservoir
WELL HILL LANE
Well Hill
ORPINGTON
HEWITTS ROAD
CHELSFIELD
Pasgalls Wood
West Wood
HOLLOWS WOOD
M25 Junction 4
Coneyearth Wood
M25
KNOCKHOLT
WHEATSHEAF HILL
BY - PASS
LONDON ROAD
CADLOCKS HILL
A224
Saunders Spring Wood
CHELSFIELD LANE
LANE

©Estate Publications

Leaves
Green

Downe

Luxted

West Kent Golf Course

Sew Wood

Snotsdale Wood

Leasons Wood

Thompson Wood

Down House

Downe School

BIGGIN HILL AIRPORT

AIRPORT IND EST
BIGGIN HILL
BUSINESS PARK
CONCORDE
BUSINESS
PARK

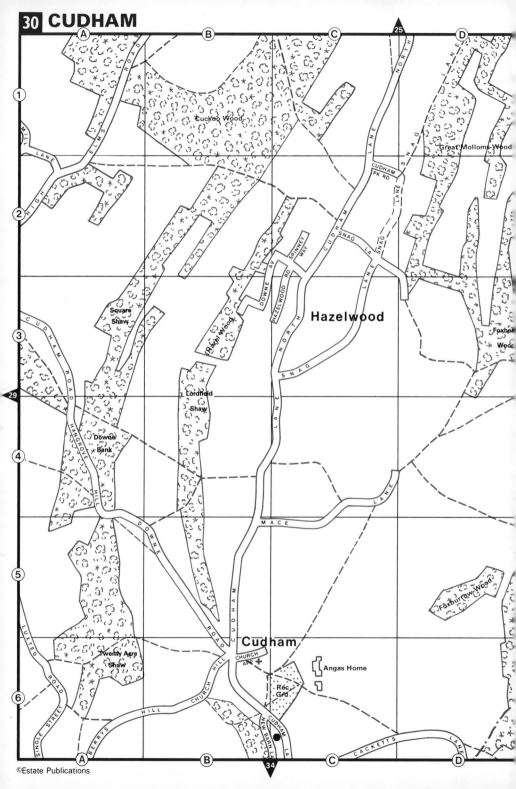

30 CUDHAM

©Estate Publications

Little Molloms Wood

Pratts Bottom

SHORTERS OASTS

ORCHARD ROAD

CHARMWOOD

RUSHMORE CL

LAMBARDES LANE

RUNCIMANWOOD

DOWNE AV

STONEHOUSE

FOXWOOD GRO

HILL

Charm Wood

Pratts Bottom School

Pratts Grove

NORSTEAD LANE

HOOKWOOD HILL

RUSHMORE ROAD

Homefield Spring

NORSTED LANE

PORT HILL LANE

BUDGINS

FAIRTROUGH

Broom Wood

High Wood

Lattice Coppice

Lower Randles Wood

HILL LANE

Karrigles Wood

ROAD

PERRYS LANE

Perry Wood

STUBBS HILL

WASHNEYS LANE

NEW YEARS LANE

Haymans Wood

Newlands Wood

Piece Wood

Newyears Wood

SINGLES CROSS LANE

LA RANDLES

POUND LANE

BLUEBERRY

Biggin Hill

Charles Darwin School
and Leisure Centre

Cudham
School

Restavon
Caravan
Site

MAGNOLIA

ACER
SPRUCE
RD
Cemetery

Biggin Hill
School

KING
GEORGE
V
AV

Recreation Ground

Fire
Station

MAPLE
LEA
CL
Lib

Youth
Centre

CHURCH

THE
RIDING

Pol
Sta

NELSON
CL

MALAN
CL

Aperfield

VILLAGE GREEN AV

Cherry Lodge Golf Course

MAIN

South
Street

MOSELLE RD

WINTFREDS

BELVEDERE

WOODBURY RD

CLARENCE RD

HILLSIDE ROAD

THE GROVE

CUDHAM ROAD

Painters Wood

ASHEN SHAW

MANOR ROAD

AVENUE

Hawleys Corner

TATSFIELD

PARKWOOD RD

PALACE RD

CHESTNUT AV

WESTERHAM HILL

A233

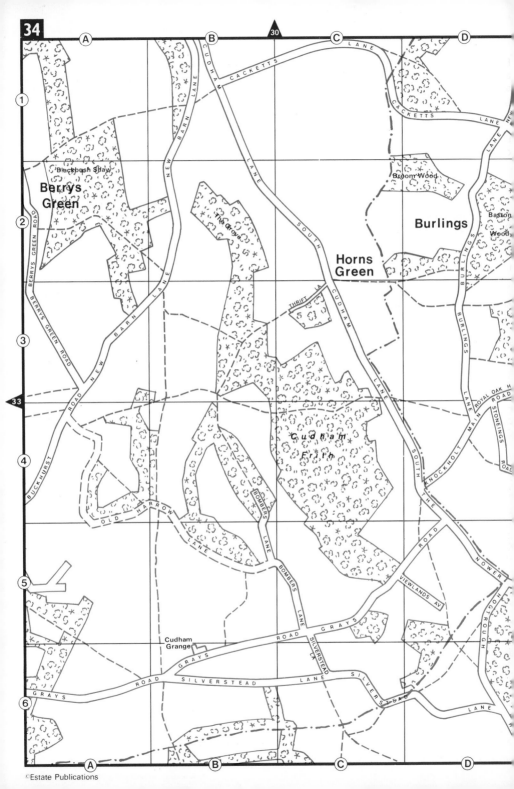

LONDON BOROUGH OF BROMLEY

Bromley Borough is an area of contrasts with rolling green fields and wooded hills in the south-east and built up areas in the north and west. Although within easy reach of central London the region has a strong identity. Bromley, Beckenham, Orpington, Penge and Chislehurst are the major towns which give the area its own special character.

It is also the largest of the London Boroughs covering around 59 square miles. The Borough lies in the south-east corner of Greater London, extending from Crystal Palace in the north-west to the border of Swanley in the east and Biggin Hill in the south.

It is predominantly residential and has small belts of light industry, modern business premises and up-to-date shopping thoroughfares.

There are good facilities for all branches of sport with swimming pools and leisure centres at Bromley, West Wickham, Beckenham and Orpington. Crystal Palace has the National Sports Centre which caters for participants and spectators. There is an athletics track at Norman Park and numerous golf courses throughout the Borough. A range of parks and nature reserves offer a selection of interesting walks.

Over 1,500 organisations, clubs and societies exist in the area together with a comprehensive adult education service which allows residents to pursue a wide range of interests.

Regular train and bus services connect all parts of the Borough with the City and West End as well as providing vital links within the region.

For further details please ring the Civic Centre on 020 8464 3333.

N.B. — This map has been carefully prepared and brought up-to-date at the time of going to press. However, ongoing development in the Borough means that work completed shortly after publication of this map will not be included. Queries concerning locations should be addressed to the Bromley Civic Centre, Stockwell Close, Bromley. BR1 3UH.

CAR PARKS — PUBLIC

Location	Capacity
BECKENHAM	
Village Way, Beckenham (multi-storey)	283
*St. George's Road, Beckenham	153
Leisure Centre, Beckenham	117
Fairfield Road, Beckenham	105
Penge East	58
Dunbar Avenue, Elmers End	67
ABC Cinema, Beckenham	55
Lennard Road, Beckenham	45
CHISLEHURST	
High Street, Chislehurst	142
Hornbrook House, High St, Chislehurst	75
Red Hill, Chislehurst	38
ST PAULS CRAY	
*Cotmandene Crescent, St. Paul's Cray	38
WEST WICKHAM	
Ravenswood Avenue, West Wickham	170
High Street, West Wickham	138
Station Road, West Wickham	76
West Wickham Pools	67
Coney Hall	26
PETTS WOOD	
Memorial Hall	52
Queensway	47

Location	Capacity
BROMLEY	
The Glades (multi-storey)	1,540
The Hill, Beckenham Lane (multi-storey)	820
Civic Centre (multi-storey) (weekends)	721
Civic Centre (multi-storey) (Mon-Fri)	521
Westmoreland Road (multi-storey)	593
Masons Hill (temporary)	143
Burnt Ash Lane	108
Palace Grove (Sat. & Sun. only)	88
Station Road (not Thursday)	79
Plaistow Lane	77
North Street (temporary)	44
South Street (Sat. & Sun. only)	54
Wharton Road	20
Crown Lane	18
*Churchill Way	4 Disabled, 2 Coach bays
ORPINGTON	
Station Road, Orpington (multi-storey)	549
College of Further Education (Saturday only)	56
Homefield Rise (15 Disabled)	15
HAYES	
Station Approach	141
BIGGIN HILL	
Lebanon Gardens	28

*Parking facilities available for commercial vehicles and coaches.

COUNCIL DEPARTMENTS

OUR MAIN SERVICES — WHO TO CONTACT

Bromley Civic Centre, Stockwell Close, Bromley BR1 3UH   020 8464 3333
www.bromley.gov.uk

Borough Secretary

Legal work
Council and Committee
  agendas and other
  records
Electoral Services
Central telephones
Enquiries
Police liaison/Community
  safety

Borough Treasurer

Council Tax
Business Rates
Housing Benefits
General financial matters
Payroll and Pensions

Chief Executive

Central personnel matters
Health and Safety
General Council
  management issues

Director of Environmental Services

Refuse collection
Roads
Sewers
Car parking
Public toilets
Traffic
Street Lighting
Environmental strategy
Recycling
Street cleansing
Planning applications
Building control
Local Land Charges
Tree preservation
Town and countryside
  improvements and
  conservation
Trading Standards
Noise nuisance
Pest control
Consumer advice
Food safety
Weights and Measures
Renovation grants
Entertainment licenses
Pollution control

Director of Education

Schools
Careers Service
Youth Service
Student awards
Adult Education
Special Educational
  Needs
Education Welfare

Director of Social Services and Housing

Social Services for
  children, families,
  elderly people and
  people with learning
  or physical disabilities
Personal Care
Foster Care
Meals Service
Inspection & Registration
Residential care
Homeless families
Social work
Occupational Therapy
Day Centres
Bus passes

Director of Leisure and Community Services

Central Library,
High Street,
Bromley BR1 1EX
Tel: 020 8460 9955

Parks and Open Spaces
Tree Maintenance
Leisure Centres
Sports facilities
Sports Development
Golf Courses
Libraries and Information
Business Information
  Service
Museum Service
Allotments
Cemeteries
Civic Halls
Arts and Entertainment
Tourism
Ecology/Nature Centres
Registration of Births,
  Deaths and Marriages
Council building
  maintenance
Architecture and Quantity
  Surveying
Land and Valuation
  Services
National Lottery projects

Please note that some services are not based at the same address as the Chief Officer.

GETTING IT RIGHT
At Bromley Council
What to do if things go wrong?

Get in touch with the Department concerned; either call in, send a letter or give us a ring.

If you are not sure who to talk to, ring 020 8464 3333 or ask at any enquiry desk. Explain the problem and they will help you to contact the right person.

A - Z INDEX TO STREETS
with Postcodes

The Index includes some names for which there is insufficient space on the maps. These names are preceded by an * and are followed by the nearest adjoining thoroughfare.

38

39

Street	Ref
Cudham La. TN14	30 C6
Cudham La Nth. BR6	25 F6
Cudham La Sth. TN14	34 B1
Cudham Park Rd. TN14	30 C2
Cudham Rd. BR6	29 H2
Cudham Rd. TN16	33 E5
Cuff Cres. SE9	4 C1
Culverstone Clo. BR2	16 D3
Cumberland Rd, Shortlands. BR2	8 D6
Cumberland Rd, Sth Norwood. SE25	14 C3
Cumberlow Av. SE25	6 B6
Cunningham Rd. BR4	16 A6
Cupola Clo. BR1	9 F1
Curtismill Clo. BR5	12 A6
Curtismill Way. BR5	12 A6
Curzon St. SE25	25 F2
Cypress St. SE25	6 A5
Cyril Rd. BR6	19 H4
D'Arcy Pl. BR2	17 E1
Daerwood Clo. BR2	18 B5
Daffodil Clo. CR0	15 E5
Dainford Clo. BR1	8 B1
Dainton Clo. BR1	9 F4
Dairy Clo. BR1	9 F3
Daisy Clo. CR0	15 E5
Dale Rd. BR8	13 H6
Dale Wood Rd. BR6	19 F4
Daleside. BR6	26 A3
Daleside Clo. BR6	26 A4
Dalmally Rd. CR0	14 A4
Dalton Clo. BR6	25 G1
Daltons Rd, Orpington. BR6	27 G2
Daltons Rd, Swanley. BR8	21 H5
Dane Clo. BR6	25 E3
Danebury. CR0	22 A4
Dargate Clo. SE19	6 A3
Darley Clo. CR0	15 E3
Darrick Wood Rd. BR6	19 E6
Dartmouth Rd. BR2	17 E4
Dartnell Rd. CR0	14 A4
Davema Clo. BR7	10 C4
Davidson Rd. CR0	14 A4
Davies Clo. CR0	14 B3
Dawell Dri. TN16	32 D2
Dawson Av. BR5	12 B5
De Lapre Clo. BR5	20 C4
Deacons Leas. BR6	25 F2
Deepdale Av. BR2	16 D2
Deer Park Way. BR4	16 D6
Degema Rd. BR6	10 D1
Delamere Cres. CR0	14 D3
Dellfield Clo. BR3	8 A4
Den Clo. BR2	8 C6
Den Rd. BR2	8 C6
Denbigh Clo. BR7	10 B2
Denbridge Rd. BR1	10 B5
Dene Clo. BR2	16 D5
Dene Dri. BR6	26 B1
Denmark Rd, Bromley. BR1	9 F4
Denmark Rd, Sth Norwood. SE25	14 B2
Dennard Way. CR0	24 C2
Densole Clo. BR3	7 F4
Denver Clo. BR6	19 G3
Derrick Rd. BR3	15 F1
Derry Downs. BR5	20 B3
Derwent Dri. BR5	19 E4
Derwent Rd. SE20	6 B5
Detling Rd. BR1	9 E1
Devonshire Rd, Mottingham. SE9	4 C4
Devonshire Rd, Orpington. BR6	19 H4
Devonshire Sq. BR2	17 F1
Devonshire Way. CR0	15 F6
Diameter Rd. BR5	18 D4
Dickens Dri. BR7	11 E2
Dickensons La. SE25	14 B3
Dittisham Rd. SE9	4 C6
Ditton Pl. SE20	6 C4
Dixon Pl. BR4	15 H5
Dixon Rd. SE25	6 A6
Doctors Clo. SE26	6 D1
Dominic Dri. SE9	5 F6
Dominion Rd. CR0	14 A4
Dorado Gdns. BR6	26 C1
Dorchester Clo. BR5	12 A3
Dorney Rise. BR5	19 H2
Dorrit Way. BR7	11 E2
Dorset Rd, Beckenham. BR3	7 E6
Dorset Rd, Mottingham. SE9	4 C4
Doveney Clo. BR5	12 C6
Doves Clo. BR2	18 A6
Dowding Rd. TN16	33 E1
Dowlerville Rd. BR6	25 H4
Downe Av. TN14	30 B3
Downe Rd, Cudham. TN14	30 B5
Downe Rd, Keston. BR6	24 A6
Downham Way. BR1	8 C1
Downleys Clo. SE9	4 D4
Downs Av. BR7	10 B1
Downs Hill. BR3	8 B4
Downs Rd. BR3	7 H5
Downs View Clo. BR6	31 H1
Downsbridge Rd. BR3	8 B4
Downsway. BR6	25 F3
Doyle Rd. SE25	14 B1
Draven Clo. BR2	16 D3
Drayton Av. BR6	18 D5
Druids Way. BR2	16 C1
Dryden Way. BR6	20 A5
Dryland Av. BR6	25 G2
Dudham Rd. TN16	33 F5
Duddington Clo. SE9	4 B5
Dudsbury Rd. DA14	12 B2
Dukes Way. BR4	22 D1
Dulverton Rd. SE9	4 C5
Dulwich Wood Av. SE19	6 A1
Dulwich Wood Pk. SE19	6 A1
Dunbar Av. BR3	15 F1
Dundee Rd. SE25	14 C2
Dunfield Gdns. SE6	8 A1
Dunfield Rd. SE6	8 A1
Dunkery Rd. SE9	4 B6
Dunley Dri. CR0	22 A5
Dunsfold Way. CR0	22 A6
Dura Den Clo. BR3	7 H3
Durban Rd. BR3	7 F5
Durham Av. BR2	16 D1
Durham Rd, Bromley. BR2	8 D6
Durham Rd, Sidcup. DA14	12 A1
Durley Gdns. BR6	26 A1
Durrant Way. BR6	25 F3
Duxberry Clo. BR2	18 A2
Dyke Dri. BR5	20 B5
Dykes Way. BR2	8 D6
Dymchurch Clo. BR6	25 G2
Eagles Dri. TN16	33 E3
Earls Way. BR6	19 H6
East Dri. BR5	20 A3
East Hall Rd. BR5	20 D4
East Hill. TN16	32 C4
East St. BR1	9 E5
East Way. BR2	17 E4
Eastbury Rd. BR5	19 F3
Eastcote. BR6	19 G5
Eastern View. TN16	32 C2
Eastmead Clo. BR1	10 A5
Eastnor Rd. SE9	5 G3
Eastry Av. BR2	17 E3
Eastwell Clo. BR3	7 F4
Ebury Clo. BR2	24 A1
Eccleston Clo. BR6	19 F5
Eden Park Av. BR3	15 F1
Eden Rd. BR3	15 E1
Eden Way. BR3	15 G2
Edenbridge Clo. BR5	20 C1
Edgar Rd. TN16	32 D6
Edgebury. BR7	5 F6
Edgehill Rd. BR7	5 G5
Edgewood Dri. BR6	25 H3
Edgewood Grn. CR0	15 E5
Edgington Way. DA14	12 B3
Edison Rd. BR2	9 E5
Edith Rd. BR6	26 A3
Edmund Rd. BR5	20 B3
Edmunds Av. BR5	12 C6
Edward Rd, Biggin Hill. TN16	33 F3
Edward Rd, Bromley. BR1	9 F3
Edward Rd, Chislehurst. BR7	10 D1
Edward Rd, Croydon. CR0	14 A4
Edward Rd, Penge. SE20	7 E3
Edward Tyler Rd. SE12	4 A4
Elborough Rd. SE25	14 B2
Elder Oak Clo. SE20	6 C4
Elderslie Clo. BR3	15 H3
Eldon Av. CR0	14 D6
Eldon Pk. SE25	14 C1
Eldred Dri. BR5	20 C5
Elgal Clo. BR6	24 D3
Elgin Rd. CR0	14 A5
Elham Clo. BR1	9 H3
Elizabeth Way. BR5	20 B2
Ellen Clo. BR1	9 H6
Ellenborough Rd. DA14	12 D2
Ellesmere Av. BR3	8 A5
Elliot Rd. BR2	17 H1
Ellis Clo. SE9	5 G3
Ellison Rd. DA15	5 H3
Elm Bank Dri. BR1	9 H5
Elm Gro. BR6	19 G5
Elm Park Rd. SE25	6 A6
Elm Rd, Beckenham. BR3	7 F5
Elm Rd, Green Street Green. BR6	25 H5
Elm Walk. BR6	24 B1
Elmcroft Rd. BR6	20 A4
Elmdene Clo. BR3	15 F3
Elmers End Rd. SE20	6 D5
Elmers Rd. SE25	14 B4
Elmerside Rd. BR3	15 F1
Elmfield Park. BR1	9 E6
Elmfield Rd. BR1	9 F6
Elmgrove Rd. CR0	14 C5
Elmhurst Rd. SE9	4 C4
Elmlee Clo. BR7	10 B2
Elmscott Rd. BR1	8 D1
Elmside. CR0	22 A4
Elmstead Av. BR7	10 B1
Elmstead Glade. BR7	10 B2
Elmstead La. BR7	10 A2
Elstan Way. CR0	15 F4
Elstree Hill. BR1	8 C3
Eltham Palace Rd. SE9	4 A1
Elvington Grn. BR2	17 E2
Elvino Rd. SE26	7 E1
Elwill Way. BR3	16 A1
Elysian Av. BR5	19 G3
Ember Clo. BR5	18 D4
Empire Sq. SE20	6 D3
Empress Dri. BR7	10 D2
Englefield Clo. BR5	19 H1
Englefield Cres. BR5	19 H1
Englefield Path. BR5	19 H1
Enmore Av. SE25	14 B2
Enmore Rd. SE25	14 B2
Enslin Rd. SE9	5 E1
Eresby Dri. BR3	15 H5
Eridge Green Clo. BR5	20 C5
Erin Clo. BR1	8 C3
Ermington Rd. SE9	5 G4
Ernest Clo. BR3	15 G2
Ernest Gro. BR3	15 G2
Escott Gdns. SE9	4 C6
Estcourt Rd. SE25	14 C3
Etfield Gro. DA14	12 A1
Ethel Ter. BR6	26 B6
Ethelbert Clo. BR1	9 E6
Ethelbert Rd, Bromley. BR1	9 E6
Ethelbert Rd, St Paul's Cray. BR5	12 C6
Eton Rd. BR6	26 A2
Eugenie Mews. BR7	10 C4
Evelina Rd. SE20	6 D3
Evening Clo. BR3	8 B3
Everard Av. BR2	17 E5
Everglade. TN16	32 D3
Everton Rd. CR0	14 B5
Evry Rd. DA14	12 C2
Exeter Rd. CR0	14 A4
Exford Rd. SE12	4 A3
Eyebright Clo. CR0	15 E5
Eynsford Clo. BR5	19 E3
Eynswood Dri. DA14	12 B1
Fair Acres. BR2	17 E2
Fair Way. BR5	19 E2
Fairbank Av. BR6	18 D6
Fairchildes Av. CR0	28 A3
Fairfield Rd, Beckenham. BR3	7 H5
Fairfield Rd, Bromley. BR1	9 E3
Fairfield Rd, Orpington. BR5	19 F3
Fairford Av. CR0	15 H2
Fairford Clo. CR0	15 E2
Fairhaven Av. CR0	15 E3
Fairlands. SE9	5 E1
Fairlawn Pk. SE26	7 F1
Fairmead. BR1	18 B1
Fairmead Clo. BR1	18 B1
Fairoak Clo. BR5	18 D4
Fairtrough Rd. BR6	31 G3
Fairview Clo. SE26	7 F1
Fairview Dri. BR6	25 F2
Fairway Clo. CR0	15 E2
Fairway Gdns. BR3	16 B3
Falcon Av. BR1	18 A1
Falcons Clo. TN16	33 E2
Faraday Way. BR5	20 A1
Faringdon Av. BR2	18 C4
Farleigh Av. BR2	17 E4
Farley Pl. SE25	14 B1
Farm Av. BR8	13 H6
Farm Clo. BR4	22 D1
Farm Dri. CR0	15 G6
Farm La. CR0	15 G6
Farmfield Rd. BR1	8 C1
Farmland Walk. BR7	10 D1
Farnaby Rd. BR1	8 C1
Farnborough Common. BR6	24 B1
Farnborough Cres. BR2	16 D5
Farnborough Hill. BR6	25 G3
Farnborough Way. BR6	24 D3
Faro Clo. BR1	10 C5
Farquhar Rd. SE19	6 A1
Farrant Clo. BR6	25 H6
Farrier Clo. BR1	9 H6
Farrington Av. BR5	12 B6
Farrington Pl. BR7	11 E3
Farthing Barn La. BR6	24 B6
Farthing St. BR6	24 B6
Farwig La. BR1	9 E4
Fashoda Rd. BR2	17 H1
Faversham Rd. BR3	7 G5
Felhampton Rd. SE9	5 F4
Felix Manor. BR7	11 F3
Felmingham Rd. SE20	6 D5
Felstead Rd. BR6	20 A4
Felton Clo. BR5	18 D3
Felton Lea. DA14	11 G5
Fenn Clo. BR1	9 E3
Fennel Clo. CR0	15 E5
Fenton Clo. BR7	10 B2
Ferguson Clo. BR2	8 B6
Fern Hill Pl. BR6	25 E1
Ferndale. BR1	9 G3
Ferndale Rd. SE25	14 C1
Ferndale Way. BR6	25 F5
Ferndown Av. BR6	19 F5
Ferndown Rd. SE9	4 B3
Fernhurst Rd. CR0	14 C5
Fernwood Clo. BR1	9 G3
Field Clo. BR1	9 G3
Field Way. CR0	22 A4
Fieldside Clo. BR6	24 D3
Fieldside Rd. BR1	8 C5
Fieldway. BR5	19 F3
Filey Clo. TN16	32 C3
Finglesham Clo. BR5	20 C5
Finucane Dri. BR5	20 C5
Fir Dene. BR6	24 B6
Fir Tree Clo. BR6	25 H5
Fire Station Mews. BR3	7 H5
Firmingers Rd. BR6	27 G3
Firsby Av. CR0	15 E5
Fisher Clo. CR0	14 A4
Fishponds Rd. BR2	23 H1
Fitzjames Av. CR0	14 C5
Five Elms Rd. BR2	23 G3
Flag Clo. CR0	15 E5
Flamborough Clo. TN16	32 C4
Fletchers Clo. BR2	17 F4
Flimwell Clo. BR1	8 C1
Flint Clo. BR6	25 G5
Flint Down Clo. BR5	11 H1
Florence Rd, Beckenham. BR3	7 E6
Florence Rd, Bromley. BR1	9 E3
Foley Rd. TN16	32 D6
Fonthill Clo. SE20	6 B5
Fontwell Dri. BR2	18 C5
Footbury Hill Rd. BR6	20 A4
Foots Cray High St. DA14	12 C2
Foots Cray Rd. SE9	5 E4
Fordcroft Rd. BR5	20 A4
Forde Av. BR1	9 G3
Fordwich Clo. BR6	19 G5

Forest Clo. BR7	10 C4	
Forest Dri. BR2	24 A2	
Forest Ridge, Beckenham. BR3	7 G6	
Forest Ridge, Keston. BR2	24 A2	
Forest Way, Avery Hill. DA15	5 H2	
Forest Way, Orpington. BR5	19 H2	
Forge Clo. BR2	17 F5	
Forgefield. TN16	32 D2	
Forstal Clo. BR2	9 E6	
Forster Rd. BR3	7 E6	
Fosters Clo. BR7	10 B1	
Fountain Dri. SE19	6 A1	
Fowler Clo. DA14	12 D1	
Fox Clo. BR6	25 H3	
Fox Hill, Keston. BR2	23 G3	
Fox Hill, Upper Norwood. SE19	6 A3	
Fox Hill Gdns. SE19	6 A3	
Fox La. BR2	23 F3	
Foxbury Av. BR7	11 F2	
Foxbury Clo, Bromley. BR1	9 F2	
Foxbury Clo, Green Street Green. BR6	25 H3	
Foxbury Dri. BR6	25 H4	
Foxbury Rd. BR1	9 F2	
Foxcombe. CR0	22 A4	
Foxearth Clo. TN16	33 F3	
Foxes Dale. BR2	8 C6	
Foxfield Rd. BR	19 E6	
Foxgrove Av. BR3	8 A3	
Foxgrove Rd. BR3	8 A3	
Foxhome Clo. BR7	10 C2	
Foxwood Gro. BR6	31 H1	
Framlingham Cres. SE9	4 D6	
Francis Rd. BR5	12 C6	
Franklin Rd. SE20	6 D3	
Frankswood Av. BR5	18 D2	
Frant Clo. SE20	6 D3	
Freelands Gro. BR1	9 F4	
Freelands Rd. BR1	9 F4	
Freesia Clo. BR6	25 G3	
Frensham Dri. CR0	22 B5	
Frensham Rd. SE9	5 H4	
Freshfields CR0	15 F5	
Freshwood Clo. BR3	7 H4	
Frewing Clo. BR7	10 B2	
Friar Rd. BR5	20 A2	
Frimley Clo. CR0	22 B5	
Frimley Ct. DA14	12 B1	
Frimley Cres. CR0	22 B5	
Frinsted Gro. BR5	20 C1	
Frognal Pl. DA14	12 A2	
Frognall Av. DA14	11 H2	
Fryston Av. CR0	14 B6	
Fuller Clo. BR6	25 H3	
Fullerton Rd. CR0	14 A4	
Furzefield Clo. BR7	10 D2	
Furzehill Sq. BR5	20 A1	
Fyfe Way. BR1	9 E5	
Fyfield Clo. BR2	16 C1	
Gainsborough Clo. BR3	7 G3	
Gaitskell Rd. SE9	5 G3	
Garden Cotts. BR5	12 C5	
Garden La. BR1	9 F2	
Garden Rd, Bromley. BR1	9 F3	
Garden Rd, Penge. SE 22	6 D4	
Garden Walk. BR3	7 G4	
Gardiner Clo. BR5	12 C5	
Garrard Clo. BR7	10 D1	
Gascoigne Rd. CR0	22 B6	
Gates Green Rd. BR4	22 D1	
Gatestone Cres. SE12	4 A2	
Genoa Rd. SE20	6 C4	
George Groves Rd. SE20	6 B4	
George La. BR2	17 F5	
Georges Clo. BR5	12 C6	
Georges Rd. TN16	33 E5	
Georgian Clo. BR2	17 F5	
Gerda Rd. SE9	5 G4	
Giggs Hill. BR5	11 H5	
Gilbert Rd. BR1	9 E3	
Gillmans Rd. BR5	20 B5	
Gilroy Way. BR5	20 B4	
Girton Rd. SE26	7 E1	
Glade Gdns. CR0	15 F4	
Glades Pl. BR1	9 E5	
Gladeside. CR0	15 E3	
Gladstone Mews. SE20	6 D3	
Gladstone Rd. BR6	25 E3	

Gladwell Rd. BR1	9 F2	
Glanfield Rd. BR3	15 G1	
Glanville Rd. BR2	9 F6	
Glassbrook Rd. SE9	4 B1	
Glassmill La. BR2	9 E5	
Glastonbury Clo. BR5	20 B5	
Glebe House Dri. BR2	17 F5	
Glebe Rd. BR1	9 E4	
Glebe Way. BR4	16 B6	
Gleeson Dri. BR6	25 G3	
Glenbow Rd. BR1	8 C2	
Glendale Mews. BR3	8 A4	
Glendower Cres. BR6	20 A3	
Gleneagles Clo. BR6	19 F5	
Gleneagles Grn. BR6	19 F5	
Glenthorne Av. CR0	14 C5	
Glentrammon Av. BR6	25 G4	
Glentrammon Clo. BR6	25 H4	
Glentrammon Gdns. BR6	25 G4	
Glentrammon Rd. BR6	25 G4	
Glenview Rd. BR1	9 H5	
Glenwood Way. CR0	15 E3	
Gload Cres. BR5	20 C6	
Glyndebourne Pk. BR6	18 D6	
Goatsfield Rd. TN16	32 D5	
Goddard Rd. BR3	15 E1	
Goddington Chase. BR6	26 A2	
Goddington La. BR6	25 H1	
Godric Cres. CR0	22 B6	
Godwin Rd. BR2	9 G6	
Goldcrest Way. CR0	22 B5	
Goldfinch Clo. BR6	26 A3	
Golf Rd. BR1	10 C6	
Goodhart Way. BR4	16 C4	
Goodhew Rd. CR0	14 B3	
Goodmead Rd. BR6	20 A4	
Goose Green Clo. BR5	12 A5	
Gordon Cres. CR0	14 A5	
Gordon Rd, Beckenham. BR3	7 F6	
Gordon Rd, Elmers End. BR3	7 E5	
Gordon Way. BR1	9 E4	
Gorse Rd. BR6	27 F1	
Gosshill Rd. BR7	10 C5	
Gossington Clo. BR7	5 F6	
Goudhurst Rd. BR1	8 D1	
Gowland Pl. BR3	7 F5	
Grace Clo. SE9	4 B5	
Graham Clo. CR0	15 G6	
Grampian Clo. BR6	19 G3	
Grand View Av. TN16	32 C2	
Grange Dri, Chislehurst. BR7	10 A2	
Grange Dri, Pratts Bottom. BR6	26 B6	
Grange Rd. BR6	19 E6	
Grangewood La. BR3	7 G2	
Grant Pl. CR0	14 A5	
Grant Rd. CR0	14 A5	
Granton Rd. DA14	12 B2	
Grasmere Av. BR6	24 C1	
Grasmere Gdns. BR6	24 D1	
Grasmere Rd, Bromley. BR1	8 D4	
Grasmere Rd, Farnborough. BR6	24 C1	
Grasmere Rd, Sth Norwood. SE25	14 C3	
Gravel Pit Way. BR6	19 H6	
Gravel Rd. BR2	18 A6	
Gravelwood Clo. BR7	5 G5	
Graveney Gro. SE20	6 D3	
Grayland Clo. BR1	9 H4	
Grays Farm Rd. BR5	12 B4	
Grays Rd. TN16	33 H6	
Great Elms Rd. BR2	17 G1	
Great Harry Dri. SE9	5 E5	
Great Thrift. BR5	19 E1	
Greatwood. BR7	10 C3	
Green Clo. BR2	8 C6	
Green Court Av. CR0	14 C6	
Green Court Gdns. CR0	14 C6	
Green Farm Clo. BR6	25 G4	
Green Gdns. BR6	25 G4	
Green Hill. BR6	29 G3	
Green La, Chislehurst. BR7	10 D1	
Green La, New Eltham. SE9	5 F2	
Green La, Penge. SE20	7 E3	
Green Way. BR2	18 A3	
Greenacres. SE9	5 E1	
Greenacres Clo. BR6	24 D2	
Greencourt Rd, Crockenhill. BR8	21 H2	
Greencourt Rd, Petts Wood. BR5	19 F2	

Greenfield Dri. BR1	9 G5	
Greenfield Gdns. BR5	19 E4	
Greenhithe Clo. DA15	5 H2	
Greenleigh Av. BR5	20 A1	
Greenmead Clo. SE25	14 B2	
Greenoak Rise. TN16	32 D3	
Greenside. BR8	13 H5	
Greenside Walk. TN16	32 C4	
Greenview Av. CR0	15 F3	
Greenway, Chislehurst. BR7	10 C1	
Greenway, Tatsfield. TN16	32 D5	
Greenways. BR3	7 H5	
Greenwood Clo. BR5	19 F3	
Gregory Clo. BR2	14 D1	
Gregory Cres. SE9	4 B2	
Gresham Rd, Beckenham. BR3	7 E5	
Gresham Rd, Sth Norwood. SE25	14 B1	
Greycot Rd. BR3	7 H1	
Greys Park Clo. BR2	23 G3	
Grice Av. TN16	28 D4	
Grocery Market Pl. SE9	4 D1	
Groom Clo. BR2	17 G1	
Grosvenor Rd, Petts Wood. BR5	19 G3	
Grosvenor Rd, Sth Norwood. SE25	14 B1	
Grosvenor Rd, West Wickham. BR4	16 A5	
Grove Clo. BR2	17 E6	
Grove Park Rd. SE9	4 B5	
Grove Rd. TN16	32 D6	
Grove Vale. BR7	10 C2	
Groveland Rd. BR3	7 F6	
Grovelands Rd. BR5	12 A3	
Gulliver Rd. DA15	5 H4	
Gumping Rd. BR5	19 E5	
Gundulph Rd. BR2	9 G6	
Gwydor Rd. BR3	7 E6	
Gwydyr Rd. BR2	9 E6	
Gwynne Av. CR0	15 E4	
Hackington Cres. BR3	7 H2	
Haddon Rd. BR5	20 C2	
Hadlow Pl. SE19	6 B3	
Haig Rd. TN16	33 E2	
Haileybury Rd. BR6	26 A2	
Hainault St. SE9	5 F3	
Hale Clo. BR6	25 E2	
Halfway St. DA15	5 H2	
Hall Dri. SE26	6 C1	
Hall View. SE9	4 B4	
Hallam Clo. BR7	10 B1	
Halons Rd. SE9	5 E1	
Ham Vw. CR0	15 F3	
Hambledon Gdns. SE25	6 A6	
Hambledown Rd. DA15	5 H2	
Hambro Av. BR2	17 E5	
Hambrook Rd. SE25	6 C6	
Hamlet Rd. SE19	6 A3	
Hammelton Rd. BR1	9 E4	
Hampden Av. BR3	7 F5	
Hampden Rd. BR3	7 F5	
Hanbury Dri. TN16	28 D4	
Hangrove Hill. BR6	30 A4	
Hannah Clo. BR3	8 A6	
Hanover Dri. BR7	5 G6	
Hanson Clo. BR3	7 H3	
Hardcastle Clo. CR0	14 B3	
Hardcourts Clo. BR4	22 A1	
Hardings La. SE20	7 E2	
Harfst Way. BR8	13 H4	
Harland Av. DA15	5 H4	
Harlands Gro. BR6	24 D2	
Harley Gdns. BR6	25 F2	
Harleyford. BR1	9 G4	
Harmony Way. BR1	9 E5	
Harriet Gdns. CR0	14 B6	
Harrington Rd. SE25	14 C1	
Harrow Gdns. BR6	26 A2	
Hart Dyke Rd. BR5	20 C5	
Hartfield Cres. BR4	23 E1	
Hartfield Gro. SE20	6 C4	
Hartfield Rd. BR4	23 E2	
Harting Rd. SE9	4 C5	
Hartington Clo. BR6	25 E3	
Hartland Way. CR0	15 E6	
Hartley Clo. BR1	10 B5	
Harton Clo. BR1	9 H4	

Harts Mead Rd. SE9	4 D3	
Harvel Clo. BR5	11 H6	
Harvest Bank Rd. BR4	23 E1	
Harvest Way. BR8	21 H4	
Harvill Rd. DA14	12 D1	
Harwood Av. BR1	9 F5	
Hassock Wood. BR2	23 H2	
Hassop Walk. SE9	4 C5	
Hastings Rd, Croydon. CR0	14 A5	
Hastings Rd, Keston Mark. BR2	18 A5	
Hathaway Clo. BR2	18 B5	
Hathern Gdns. SE9	5 E6	
Havelock Rd, Addiscombe. CR0	14 A5	
Havelock Rd, Bromley. BR2	17 G1	
Haven Clo. SE9	4 D5	
Haven Rd. DA14	12 B2	
Haverthwaite Rd. BR6	19 F6	
Hawes La. BR4	16 B5	
Hawes Rd. BR1	9 F4	
Hawfield Bank. BR6	26 C1	
Hawkeshead Clo. BR1	8 D3	
Hawkhurst Way. BR4	16 A6	
Hawkinge Walk. BR5	12 B6	
Hawkins Way. SE6	7 H1	
Hawksbrook La. BR3	16 A3	
Hawkwood La. BR7	11 E4	
Hawstead La. BR6	27 E3	
Hawthorn Clo. BR5	19 F3	
Hawthorn Dri. BR4	22 D2	
Hawthorn Gro. SE20	6 C4	
Hawthorndene Clo. BR2	17 E6	
Hawthorndene Rd. BR2	17 E6	
Hawthorne Av. TN16	33 E1	
Hawthorne Clo. BR1	10 B6	
Hawthorne Rd. BR1	10 A6	
Haxted Rd. BR1	9 F4	
Haydens Clo. BR5	20 B3	
Hayes Chase. BR4	16 C3	
Hayes Clo. BR2	17 E6	
Hayes Gdn. BR2	17 E6	
Hayes Hill. BR2	16 C5	
Hayes Hill Rd. BR2	16 D5	
Hayes La, Beckenham. BR3	8 A6	
Hayes La, Hayes. BR2	17 F2	
Hayes Mead Rd. BR2	16 D5	
Hayes Rd. BR2	17 E1	
Hayes St. BR2	17 F5	
Hayes Way. BR3	16 A1	
Hayes Wood Av. BR2	17 F5	
Hayesford Park Dri. BR2	17 E2	
Hayfield Rd. BR5	20 A2	
Hayne Rd. BR3	7 G5	
Haysleigh Gdns. SE20	6 B5	
Haywood Rise. BR6	25 G3	
Haywood Rd. BR2	17 H1	
Hazel Clo. CR0	15 E5	
Hazel Gro, Orpington. BR6	18 C6	
Hazel Gro, Upper Sydenham. SE26	7 E1	
Hazel Walk. BR2	18 C3	
Hazelhurst. BR3	8 B4	
Hazelmere Rd. BR5	19 E1	
Hazelmere Way. BR2	17 E3	
Hazelwood Rd. TN14	30 C3	
Headcorn Rd. BR1	9 E1	
Headley Dri. BR6	25 H1	
Healey Dri. BR6	25 H1	
Hearns Rise. BR5	20 C1	
Hearns Rd. BR5	20 B1	
Heath Clo. BR5	20 B3	
Heath Gro. SE20	6 D3	
Heath Park Dri. BR1	10 A6	
Heath Rise. BR2	17 E3	
Heath Side. BR5	19 E4	
Heatherbank. BR7	10 C5	
Heathfield. BR7	11 E2	
Heathfield Clo. BR2	23 G3	
Heathfield Rd. BR7	10 D2	
Heathfield Rd, Bromley. BR1	8 D3	
Heathfield Rd, Keston. BR2	23 G3	
Heathley End. BR7	11 E2	
Heathwood Gdns. BR8	13 H5	
Helegan Clo. BR6	25 H2	
Henderson Rd. TN16	28 D3	
Hengist Rd. SE12	4 A2	
Hengist Way. BR2	16 C1	
Henry Cooper Way. SE9	4 B5	
Henry St. BR1	9 F4	
Henson Clo. BR6	18 D6	

Henville Rd. BR1	9 G4
Hepburn Gdns. BR2	16 D5
Herbert Rd. BR2	18 A2
Heritage Hill. BR2	23 G3
Hermitage La. SE25	14 B4
Heron Court. BR2	17 G1
Hesiers Hill. CR6	32 A2
Hesiers Rd. CR6	32 A2
Hetley Gdns. SE19	6 A3
Hever Croft. SE9	5 E6
Hever Gdns. BR1	10 C5
Hewitts Rd. BR6	27 E5
High Beeches, Chelsfield. BR6	26 A4
High Beeches, Foots Cray. DA14	12 D1
High Broom Cres. BR4	16 A4
High Elms Rd. BR6	24 D6
High Grove. BR1	9 G4
High Mead. BR4	16 C6
High Point. SE9	5 F5
High St, Beckenham. BR3	7 G5
High St, Bromley. BR1	9 E5
High St, Chislehurst. BR7	10 D2
High St, Downe. BR6	29 H2
High St, Farnborough. BR6	24 D3
High St, Green Street Green. BR6	25 G4
High St, Orpington. BR6	19 H5
High St, Penge. SE20	6 C2
High St, St Mary Cray. BR5	20 B3
High St, Sth Norwood. SE25	6 B6
High St, West Wickham. BR4	16 A5
High Tor. BR1	9 F4
High Trees. CR0	15 F5
High View Clo. SE19	6 A5
High View Rd. BR6	29 H1
Highams Hill. TN16	28 B3
Highbarrow Rd. CR0	14 B5
Highbury Clo. BR4	16 A6
Highcombe Clo. SE9	4 C3
Highfield Av. BR6	25 H3
Highfield Dri, Bromley. BR2	16 D1
Highfield Dri, West Wickham. BR4	22 A1
Highfield Rd, Biggin Hill. TN16	32 C2
Highfield Rd, Bromley. BR1	18 B1
Highfield Rd, St Paul's Cray. BR5	11 G6
Highgrove Clo. BR1	10 A4
Highgrove Ct. BR3	7 G3
Highland Croft. BR3	7 H2
Highland Rd. BR1	8 D4
Highlands Rd. BR5	20 B4
Highview. BR7	10 B3
Highwood Dri. BR6	19 E6
Highwood Dri. BR6	18 D6
Hilborough Way. BR6	25 F3
Hilda Vale Clo. BR6	24 C2
Hilda Vale Rd. BR6	24 C2
Hildenborough Gdns. BR1	8 D2
Hildenlea Pl. BR2	8 C5
Hill Brow. BR1	9 H4
Hill Clo. BR7	10 C1
Hill Crest Rd. TN16	32 D1
Hill End. BR6	19 H6
Hill House Mews. BR2	9 E5
Hillbrow Rd. BR1	8 C3
Hillcrest Clo, Upper Elmers End. BR3	15 F3
Hillcrest Clo, Upper Sydenham. SE26	6 B1
Hillcrest Rd, Bromley. BR1	9 E1
Hillcrest Rd, Orpington. BR6	20 A6
Hillcrest View. BR3	15 F3
Hilldown Rd. BR2	16 D5
Hilldrop Rd. BR1	9 F2
Hillingdale. TN16	32 C3
Hillmore Gro. SE26	7 E1
Hillside La. BR2	16 D6
Hillside Rd, Bromley. BR2	8 D6
Hillside Rd, Tatsfield. TN16	33 F5
Hilltop Gdns. BR6	19 F6
Hillview Cres. BR6	19 G5
Hillview Rd, Chislehurst. BR7	10 C1
Hillview Rd, Orpington. BR6	19 G5
Hinton Clo. SE9	4 D3
Hoblands End. BR7	11 G2
Hockenden La. BR8	13 F6
Hodsoll Ct. BR5	20 C2
Hodson Cres. BR5	20 C2
Holbrook La. BR7	11 F3
Holbrook Way. BR2	18 B3
Holland Clo. BR2	16 D6
Holland Rd. SE25	14 B2
Holland Way. BR2	16 D6
Holligrave Rd. BR1	9 E4
Hollingworth Rd. BR5	18 D4
Holly Clo. BR8	16 A1
Holly Cres. BR3	15 G2
Holly Rd. BR6	25 H5
Hollybrake Clo. BR7	11 E3
Hollybush La. BR6	27 F4
Hollydale Dri. BR2	24 B1
Holmbury Pk. BR1	10 A3
Holmcroft Way. BR2	18 B2
Holmdale Rd. BR7	10 D1
Holmdene Clo. BR3	8 A5
Holmesdale Rd. SE25	14 A1
Holwood Park Av. BR6	24 B2
Holywell Clo. BR6	25 H2
Home Lea. BR6	25 G3
Homecroft Rd. SE26	6 D1
Homefield Clo. BR5	20 B1
Homefield Mews. BR3	7 G4
Homefield Rise. BR6	19 H5
Homefield Rd. BR1	9 G4
Homemead Rd. BR2	18 B2
Homer Rd. CR0	15 E3
Homesdale Rd, Bromley. BR2	9 G6
Homesdale Rd, Orpington. BR5	19 F4
Homestead Rd. BR6	26 A5
Homestead Way. CR0	28 A3
Homewood Cres. BR7	11 F3
Honeybourne Way. BR5	19 E5
Honeyden Rd. DA14	12 D2
Honeysuckle Gdns. CR0	15 E5
Hood Av. BR5	20 A2
Hook Farm Rd. BR2	17 G2
Hookwood Rd. BR6	31 H2
Hope Park. BR1	8 D3
Horley Rd. SE9	4 C5
Hornbeam Way. BR2	18 C3
Horning Clo. SE9	4 D5
Horsa Rd. SE12	4 A2
Horsecroft Clo. BR6	20 A5
Horsell Rd. BR5	12 A4
Horsley Dri. CR0	22 A5
Horsley Rd. BR1	9 F4
Horsmonden Clo. BR6	19 G4
Howard Rd, Bromley. BR1	9 E3
Howard Rd, Penge. SE20	6 D4
Howard Rd, Sth Norwood. SE25	14 B2
Howards Crest Clo. BR3	8 B5
Howden Rd. SE25	6 A5
Hudson Gdns. BR6	25 G4
Hunters Gro. BR6	24 D2
Huntley Rd. SE25	14 A1
Hunts Mead Clo. BR7	10 B4
Huron Clo. BR6	25 G4
Hurst Clo. BR2	16 D5
Hurstdene Av. BR2	16 D5
Hurstfield. BR2	17 E2
Hurstwood Dri. BR1	10 B6
Husseywell Cres. BR2	17 E5
Hyde Dri. BR5	20 A1
Hythe Clo. BR5	20 B1
Ickleton Rd. SE9	4 D6
Iden Clo. BR2	8 C6
Imperial Pl. BR7	10 C4
Imperial Way. BR7	5 G5
Inca Dri. SE9	5 F2
Inchwood. BR4	22 A2
INDUSTRIAL & RETAIL:	
Airport Ind Est. TN16	29 E6
Beckenham Business Centre. BR3	7 F2
Biggin Hill Business Park. TN16	29 E6
Broomsleigh Business Park. SE26	7 G1
Concorde Business Park. TN16	29 E6
Crayfield Business Pk. BR5	12 B4
Crayfield Ind Park. BR5	12 C5
Franklin Ind Est. SE20	6 D4
Kangley Business Centre. SE26	7 F1
Metro Business Centre. SE26	7 G1
Murray Business Centre. BR5	12 B6
Nugent Ind Park. BR5	20 B2
Orpington Retail Pk. BR5	20 B1
Orchard Business Centre. SE26	7 F1
Ravensquay Business Centre. BR5	20 B2
Sidcup Tech Centre. DA14	12 C2
Springvale Retail Pk. BR5	12 B6
Station Estate. BR3	15 E1
The Arthur Ruxley Est. DA14	12 C2
Ingatestone Rd. SE25	14 C2
Ingleby Way. BR7	10 C1
Ingleside Clo. BR3	7 G3
Inglewood Copse. BR1	10 A5
Inglis Rd. CR0	14 A5
Inspirations Way. BR6	19 H4
Invicta Clo. BR7	10 C1
Inwood Clo. CR0	15 F6
Irene Rd. BR6	19 H4
Iris Clo. CR0	15 E5
Irvine Way, Orpington. BR6	19 G4
Irvine Way, Swanley. BR8	13 H5
Isabella Dri. BR6	24 D2
Islehurst Clo. BR7	10 C4
Ivers Way. CR0	22 A5
Ivor Gro. SE9	5 F3
Ivychurch Clo. SE20	6 C3
Jackass La. BR2	23 F4
Jackson Rd. BR2	18 A6
Jaffray Rd. BR2	17 H1
Jail La. TN16	33 F1
Jasmine Clo. BR6	18 C6
Jasmine Gro. SE20	6 C4
Jason Wk. SE9	5 E5
Jasper Rd. SE19	6 A2
Jay Gdns. BR7	4 D6
Jenson Way. SE19	6 A3
Jersey Dri. BR5	19 E3
Jesmond Rd. CR0	14 A4
Jevington Way. SE12	4 A3
Jewels Hill. TN16	28 B4
Joan Cres. SE9	4 C2
John St. SE25	14 B1
Johns Rd. TN16	32 D5
Johnson Rd. BR2	17 H2
Jubilee Rd. BR6	27 F4
Jug Hill. TN16	32 D1
Juglans Rd. BR6	19 H5
Julian Rd. BR6	26 A4
Juniper Clo. TN16	33 F2
Kangley Bridge Rd. SE26	7 G1
Karen Ct. BR1	8 D4
Keats Way. CR0	14 D3
Kechill Gdns. BR2	17 E4
Kedleston Dri. BR5	19 G3
Keedonwood Rd. BR1	8 C1
Keightley Dri. SE9	5 G3
Keith Park Cres. TN16	28 D4
Kelby Path. SE9	5 F5
Kelsey La. BR3	7 G6
Kelsey Park Av. BR3	8 A5
Kelsey Park Rd. BR3	7 H5
Kelsey Rd. BR5	12 B5
Kelsey Sq. BR3	7 G5
Kelsey Way. BR3	7 G6
Kelvin Par. BR6	19 F5
Kelvington Clo. CR0	15 F4
Kemble Dri. BR2	24 A1
Kembleside Rd. TN16	32 C3
Kemerton Rd, Beckenham. BR3	8 A5
Kemerton Rd, Croydon. CR0	14 A4
Kemnal Rd. BR7	11 E2
Kempton Wk. CR0	15 F3
Kemsing Clo. BR2	17 E6
Kemsley Rd. TN15	32 D4
Kendale Rd. BR1	8 C1
Kendall Av. BR3	7 F5
Kendall Rd. BR3	7 F5
Kenilworth Rd, Penge. SE20	7 E4
Kenilworth Rd, Petts Wood. BR5	19 E3
Kenley Clo. BR5	11 G6
Kennedy Clo. BR5	19 E5
Kent Clo. BR6	25 G4
Kent House La. BR3	7 F2
Kent House Rd. BR3	7 E4
Kent House Station Approach. BR3	7 E4
Kent Rd, St Mary Cray. BR5	20 B3
Kent Rd, West Wickham. BR4	16 A5
Kentish Way. BR1	9 F5
Kenwood Dri. BR3	8 A6
Kersey Gdns. SE9	4 C6
Keston Av. BR2	23 G3
Keston Fruit Farm Cotts. BR2	23 G6
Keston Gdns. BR2	23 G3
Keston Park Clo. BR2	24 B1
Kestrel Way. CR0	22 B6
Keswick Rd, Orpington. BR6	19 H5
Keswick Rd, West Wickham. BR4	16 C6
Kevington Clo. BR5	19 H1
Kevington Dri. BR5	19 G1
Keymer Clo. TN16	32 D1
Killewarren Way. BR5	20 B4
Kimberley Gate. BR1	8 D3
Kimberley Rd. BR3	7 E5
Kimmeridge Gdns. SE9	4 C6
Kimmeridge Rd. SE9	4 C6
King George VI Av. TN16	33 E2
King Henrys Dri. CR0	22 A6
King Henrys Mws. BR6	25 G3
King Johns Walk. SE9	4 B3
King Johns Walk. SE9	4 C2
King and Queen Clo. SE9	4 D6
Kingcup Clo. CR0	15 E5
Kingfisher Clo. BR5	20 C1
Kingfisher Way. BR3	15 E2
Kings Av. BR1	8 D2
Kings Hall Rd. BR3	7 E3
Kings Orchard. SE9	4 D1
Kings Rd, Biggin Hill. TN16	32 D1
Kings Rd, Orpington. BR6	25 G2
Kings Rd, Sth Norwood. SE25	6 B6
Kingscote Rd. CR0	14 C4
Kingsdale Rd. SE20	7 E4
Kingsdown Way. BR2	17 E3
Kingsgate Clo. BR5	12 B6
Kingsground. SE9	4 C2
Kingsleigh Walk. BR2	16 D1
Kingsley Mews. BR7	10 D2
Kingsley Rd. BR6	25 G5
Kingsley Wood Dri. SE9	4 D5
Kingsmead. TN16	33 E1
Kingston Cres. BR3	7 G4
Kingsway, Orpington. BR5	19 E2
Kingsway, West Wickham. BR4	22 D1
Kingswood Av. BR2	16 C1
Kingswood Clo. BR6	19 F4
Kingswood Rd, Penge. SE20	6 D2
Kingswood Rd, Shortlands. BR2	8 C6
Kingsworth Clo. BR3	15 F2
Kinnaird Av. BR1	8 D2
Kinnaird Clo. BR1	8 D2
Kippington Dri. SE9	4 C3
Kirkstone Way. BR1	8 D3
Kitley Gdns. SE19	6 A4
Knighton Park Rd. SE26	7 E1
Knights Ridge. BR6	26 B3
Knockholt Main Rd. TN14	30 A2
Knole Clo. CR0	14 D3
Knoll Rise. BR6	19 G5
Knoll Rd. DA14	12 B1
Knowle Rd. BR2	18 A6
Knowlton Grn. BR2	17 E2
Koonowla Clo. TN16	33 E1
Kydbrook Clo. BR5	19 E4
Kynaston Rd, Bromley. BR1	9 E1
Kynaston Rd, St Mary Cray. BR5	20 B4
La Tourne Gdns. BR6	25 E
Laburnum Av. BR8	13 H4
Laburnum Ct. SE19	6 A4

42

Name	Ref	Name	Ref	Name	Ref	Name	Ref
.aburnum Gdns. CR0	15 E5	Lennard Clo. BR4	16 D6	Lower Rd. BR5	20 B3	Manor Way,	
.aburnum Way. BR2	18 C4	Lennard Rd, Bromley		Loxley Clo. SE26	7 E1	Beckenham. BR3	7 H5
.adycroft Gdns. BR6	25 E3	Common. BR2	18 B5	Loxwood Clo. BR5	20 C6	Manor Way,	
.adycroft Way. BR6	24 D3	Lennard Rd, Penge. SE20	6 D2	Lubbock Rd. BR7	10 B3	Petts Wood. BR5	19 E2
.adysmith Rd. SE9	5 E1	Leof Cres. SE6	7 H1	Lucas Rd. SE20	6 D2	Manor Way,	
.adywood Av. BR5	19 G2	Letchworth Clo. BR2	17 E2	Lucerne Rd. BR6	19 H5	Southborough. BR2	18 A3
.agoon Rd. BR5	20 B2	Letchworth Dri. BR2	17 E2	Ludlow Clo. BR2	9 E6	Manorfields Clo. BR5	11 G6
.ake Av. BR1	9 E2	Leverholme Gdns. SE9	5 E5	Luffman Rd. SE12	4 A5	Mansfield Clo. BR5	20 C4
.ake Rd. CR0	15 G6	Lewes Rd. BR1	9 H5	Lullarook Clo. TN16	32 C2	Manston Clo. SE20	6 D4
.akefield Clo. SE20	6 C3	Lewing Clo. BR6	19 F5	Lullingstone Clo. BR5	12 A3	Maple Clo. BR5	19 F2
.akes Rd. BR2	23 G3	Lewis Rd. BR1	17 E3	Lullingstone Cres. BR5	12 A3	Maple Leaf Clo. TN16	33 E2
.akeside. BR3	8 A6	Leydenhatch La. BR8	13 H4	Lullington Garth. BR1	8 D3	Maple Rd. SE20	6 C4
.akeside Clo. SE25	6 B5	Leysdown Rd. SE9	4 C4	Lullington Rd. SE20	6 B3	Mapledale Av. CR0	14 B6
.akeside Dri. BR2	24 A1	Lezayre Rd. BR6	25 G4	Lulworth Rd. SE9	4 C4	Mapledene. BR7	11 E1
.akeswood Rd. BR5	18 D3	Lichlade Clo. BR6	25 G2	Lunar Clo. TN16	33 E1	Mapleton Clo. BR2	17 E2
.ambarde Av. SE9	5 E6	Liddon Rd. BR1	9 G6	Lupin Clo. CR0	15 E5	Marbrook Ct. SE12	4 A5
.ambardes Clo. BR6	31 G2	Lillie Rd. TN16	32 D3	Lushington Rd. SE6	7 H1	Marcellina Way. BR6	25 G1
.amberhurst Rd. BR5	20 C5	Lime Clo. BR1	18 A1	Lusted Hall La. TN16	32 C5	Mardell Rd. CR0	15 E2
.ambert Clo. TN16	32 D1	Lime Gro. BR6	18 D6	Luxfield Rd. SE9	4 C3	Marden Av. BR2	17 E3
.ambscroft Av. SE9	4 B5	Lime Tree Wk. BR4	22 D2	Luxted Rd. BR6	29 H3	Marechal Niel Av. DA15	5 H4
.amorna Clo. BR6	19 H4	Limes Av. SE20	6 C3	Lychgate Rd. BR6	20 A5	Margaret Gardner Dri. SE9	4 D7
.ancaster Clo. BR2	16 D1	Limes Rd. BR3	8 A5	Lyconby Gdns. CR0	15 F4	Marigold Way. CR0	15 E5
.ancaster Rd. SE25	6 A5	Limes Row. BR6	24 D3	Lydsted Rd. SE9	5 E6	Marina Clo. BR2	9 E6
.ancing Rd. BR6	20 A6	Limewood Clo. BR3	16 A2	Lymer Av. SE19	6 A1	Marion Cres. BR5	20 A4
.andsdowne Av. BR6	18 D5	Lincoln Clo. SE25	14 B3	Lynden Way. BR8	13 H6	Marke Clo. BR6	24 A2
.andsdowne Rd. BR1	9 F3	Lincoln Green Rd. BR5	19 H2	Lyndhurst Clo. BR6	24 D2	Market Meadow &	
.aneside. BR7	10 D1	Lincoln Rd, Sidcup. DA14	12 A1	Lynmouth Rise. BR5	20 A1	William Pl. BR5	20 B1
.angdale Clo. BR6	24 D1	Lincoln Rd,		Lynne Clo. BR6	25 G4	Market Sq. BR1	9 E5
.angdon Rd. BR2	9 F6	Sth Norwood. SE25	6 C6	Lynstead Ct. BR3	7 F5	Markwell Clo. BR4	16 D6
.angdon Shaw. DA14	11 G1	Linden Clo. BR6	25 H3	Lynsted Clo. BR1	9 G5	Marlborough Clo. BR6	19 G4
.angham Park Pl. BR2	16 D1	Linden Clo. SE26	6 D2	Lynton Av. BR5	20 A1	Marlborough Rd. BR2	17 G1
.anglands Gdns. CR0	15 G6	Linden Leas. BR4	16 B6	Lynwood Gro. BR6	19 G4	Marlings Clo. BR5	19 G1
.angley Gdns. Bromley. BR2	17 G1	Lindenfield. BR7	10 D5	Lyoth Rd. BR5	19 E6	Marlings Park Av. BR5	19 G1
.angley Gdns,		Lindfield Rd. CR0	14 A3	Lysander Way. BR6	25 E1	Marlow Clo. SE20	6 C6
Petts Wood. BR5	18 D3	Lindsey Clo. BR1	9 H6	Lytchet Rd. BR1	9 F3	Marlow Rd. SE20	6 C6
.angley Rd. BR3	15 E1	Link Way. BR2	18 A4			Marlowe Clo. BR7	11 E3
.angley Way. BR4	16 C5	Linkfield. BR2	17 E3	Maberley Cres. SE19	6 B3	Maroon Way. SE6	7 H1
.ankton Rd. BR3	8 A4	Links Rd. BR4	16 B5	Maberley Rd,		Marsden Way. BR6	25 G2
.annoy Rd. SE9	5 G3	Links Way. BR3	15 H3	Beckenham. BR3	7 E6	Marsham Clo. BR7	10 C1
.ansdowne Pl. SE19	6 A3	Lisleade Rd. BR6	25 H4	Maberley Rd,		Martindale Av. BR6	25 H3
.apworth Rd. BR6	20 B6	Lions Clo. SE9	4 B5	Upper Norwood. SE19	6 B4	Martins Clo,	
.arch Dene. BR6	18 C6	Liskeard Clo. BR7	11 E2	Macclesfield Rd. SE25	14 C2	St Paul's Cray. BR5	12 C6
.arch Way. BR2	18 C4	Little Acre. BR3	7 H6	Mace La. TN14	30 B5	Martins Clo,	
.archwood Rd. SE9	5 F4	Little Brook Clo. CR0	15 E3	Mackenzie Rd. BR3	6 D5	West Wickham. BR4	16 C6
.arkfield Clo. BR2	17 E6	Little Court. BR4	16 C6	Mada Rd. BR6	24 D1	Martins Rd. BR2	8 D5
.arkspur Clo. BR6	20 B6	Little Mede. SE9	4 D5	Maddocks Clo. DA14	12 D2	Marvels Clo. SE12	4 A4
.atham Clo. TN16	32 C2	Little Redlands. BR1	10 A5	Madeira Av. BR1	8 C3	Marvels La. SE12	4 A4
.aurel Gro. SE20	6 C3	Little Thrift. BR5	18 D1	Madeline Rd. SE20	6 B4	Masefield View. BR6	24 D1
.aurier Rd. CR0	14 A4	Little Wood Clo. BR5	11 H4	Madison Gdns. BR2	9 E6	Masons Hill. BR2	9 F6
.avender Clo. BR2	18 A3	Littlejohn Rd. BR5	20 A3	Maesmaur Rd. TN16	32 D6	Matfield Clo. BR2	17 E2
.avender Hill. BR8	13 H6	Littlestone Clo. BR3	7 H2	Magdalen Gro. BR6	26 A2	Mavelstone Clo. BR1	10 A4
.avender Way. CR0	15 E3	Lloyds Way. BR3	15 F2	Magnolia Dri. TN16	33 E1	Mavelstone Rd. BR1	9 H4
.avidge Rd. SE9	4 D4	Lockesley Dri. BR5	19 H3	Magpie Hall Clo. BR2	18 A4	Maxwell Gdns. BR6	25 G1
.awn Clo, Bromley. BR1	9 F3	Lockie Pl. SE25	6 B6	Magpie Hall La. BR2	18 A4	May Av. BR5	20 A2
.awn Clo, Swanley. BR8	13 H5	Lodge Clo. BR6	20 A5	Maidstone Rd. DA14	12 C2	Maybourne Clo. SE26	6 C2
.awn Rd. BR3	7 G3	Lodge Cres. BR6	20 A5	Main Rd, Biggin Hill. TN16	32 D1	Maybury Clo. BR5	18 D2
.awrence Rd,		Lodge Gdns. BR3	15 G2	Main Rd, Crockenhill. BR8	21 H3	Mayeswood Rd. SE12	4 A5
Sth Norwood. SE25	14 A1	Lodge La. CR0	22 A5	Main Rd,		Mayfare Clo. BR3	7 H4
.awrence Rd,		Lodge Rd. BR1	9 G3	St Paul's Cray. BR5	12 B4	Mayfield Av. BR6	19 G5
West Wickham. BR4	23 E2	Logs Hill. BR7	10 A4	Main Rd, Sidcup. DA14	5 H5	Mayfield Rd. BR1	18 A2
.awrie Park Av. SE26	6 C1	Logs Hill Clo. BR7	10 A4	Mainridge Rd. BR7	5 E6	Mayfly Clo. BR5	20 C1
.awrie Park Cres. SE26	6 C1	Lomas Clo. CR0	22 B5	Maitland Rd. SE26	7 E2	Mayford Clo. BR3	7 E6
.awrie Park Gdns. SE26	6 C1	London La. BR1	8 D3	Malan Clo. TN16	33 E2	Mayow Rd. SE26	7 E1
.awrie Park Rd. SE26	6 C2	London Rd, Bromley. BR1	8 D3	Malcolm Rd, Penge. SE20	6 D3	Maypole Rd. BR6	27 E3
.axey Rd. BR6	25 G4	London Rd, Swanley. BR8	13 H5	Malcolm Rd,		Mays Hill Rd. BR2	8 C5
.ayhams Rd. BR4	22 C2	Long Acre. BR6	20 C6	Sth Norwood. SE25	14 B3	Maywood Clo. BR3	7 H3
.ayzell Walk. SE9	4 C3	Long La. CR0	14 C3	Mallard Walk. BR3	15 E2	Mead Rd. BR7	10 D2
.ea Rd. BR3	7 H5	Long Meadow Clo. BR4	16 B4	Mallow Clo. CR0	14 D3	Mead Way, Hayes. BR2	16 D3
.eafy Gro. BR2	23 G3	Longbury Clo. BR5	12 A6	Malling Way. BR2	16 D4	Mead Way,	
.eafy Oak Rd. SE12	4 A5	Longbury Dri. BR5	12 A6	Malmains Clo. BR3	16 B1	West Wickham. CR0	15 F6
.eafy Way. CR0	14 A6	Longcroft. SE9	5 E5	Malmains Way. BR3	16 B1	Meadow Av. CR0	15 E3
.eamington Av,		Longdon Wood. BR6	24 A2	Maltby Clo. BR6	19 H5	Meadow Clo,	
Bromley. BR1	9 G1	Longfield. BR1	9 E4	Malvern Clo. SE20	6 B5	Chislehurst. BR7	10 D1
.eamington Av,		Longheath Gdns. CR0	14 D2	Malvern Rd. BR6	26 A2	Meadow Clo,	
Orpington. BR6	25 F2	Longhurst Rd. CR0	14 C3	Manitoba Gdns. BR6	25 G4	Lwr Sydenham. SE6	7 H1
.eamington Clo. BR1	9 G1	Longlands Park Cres. DA15	5 H4	Manning Rd. BR5	20 C2	Meadow Rd. BR2	8 D5
.eas Dale. SE9	5 E5	Longleat Mews. BR5	20 B1	Manor Gro. BR3	7 H5	Meadow View. BR5	12 B6
.eas Grn. BR7	11 G2	Longmead. BR7	10 C5	Manor Park. BR7	11 E5	Meadow Way. BR6	24 C1
.eaveland Clo. BR3	15 H1	Lonsdale Clo. SE9	4 B5	Manor Park Clo. BR4	16 A5	Meadowcroft. BR1	10 B6
.eaves Green Cres. BR2	29 E2	Lonsdale Rd. SE25	14 C1	Manor Park Rd,		Meadowview Rd. SE6	7 H1
.eaves Green Rd. BR2	23 H6	Loop Rd. BR7	10 D2	Chislehurst. BR7	11 E4	Meadside Clo. BR3	7 F4
.ebanon Gdns. TN16	33 E2	Lorne Av. CR0	15 E4	Manor Park Rd,		Meadvale Rd. CR0	14 A4
.edrington Rd. SE19	6 B2	Lorne Gdns. CR0	15 E4	West Wickham. BR4	16 A5	Meadway. BR3	8 B4
.eeds Clo. BR6	20 C6	Lotus Rd. TN16	33 F3	Manor Pl. BR7	11 E5	Meaford Way. SE20	6 C3
.eesons Hill. BR5	11 G6	Love La. SE25	6 C6	Manor Rd, Beckenham. BR3	7 H5	Meath Clo. BR5	20 A2
.eesons Hill. BR5	11 G5	Lovelace Av. BR2	18 C3	Manor Rd,		Medway Clo. CR0	14 D3
.eigh Cres, CR0	22 A5	Lovibonds Av. BR6	24 D2	Sth Norwood. SE25	6 B6	Melanda Clo. BR7	10 B1
.eith Hill. BR5	11 H4	Lower Addiscombe Rd.		Manor Rd, Tatsfield. TN16	33 E5	Melbourne Clo,	
.eith Hill Grn. BR5	11 H4	CR0	14 A5	Manor Rd,		Orpington. BR6	19 G4
.emay Rd. SE12	4 A5	Lower Camden. BR7	10 B3	West Wickham. BR4	15 H6	Melbourne Clo, Penge. SE20	6 B3
.ennard Av. BR4	16 D6	Lower Gravel Rd. BR2	18 A5	Manor View. BR3	7 G5	Melbury Clo. BR7	10 A2

Meldrum Clo. BR5 20 C3
Mells Cres. SE9 4 D6
Melody Rd. TN16 32 C4
Melrose Cres. BR6 25 F3
Melrose Rd. TN16 32 D1
Melvin Rd. SE20 6 D4
Merchland Rd. SE9 5 G3
Mere Clo. BR6 18 C6
Mere End. CR0 15 E4
Mere Side. BR6 18 C6
Merewood Clo. BR1 10 C5
Mereworth Clo. BR2 16 D2
Meriden Clo. BR1 9 H4
Merlewood Dri. BR7 10 B4
Merlin Gro. BR3 15 G1
Merrow Way. CR0 22 B5
Merrydown Way. BR7 10 A4
Merryhills Clo. TN16 32 D2
Mersham Pl. SE20 6 C4
Merton Gdns. BR5 18 D2
Merton Rd. SE25 14 B2
Mervyn Av. SE9 5 G4
Messeter Pl. SE9 5 E1
Mewsend. TN16 32 D3
Mickleham Clo. BR5 11 H5
Mickleham Rd. BR5 11 H4
Mickleham Way. CR0 22 B5
Middle Park Av. SE9 4 B1
Middleton Av. DA14 12 B2
Midfield Way. BR5 11 H4
Milestone Rd. SE19 6 A2
Milford Gdns. CR0 14 D2
Milk St. BR1 9 F2
Milking La. TN16 29 E3
Mill Brook Rd. BR5 20 B1
Mill La. BR6 29 H1
Mill Pl. BR7 10 C4
Mill Vale. BR2 9 E5
Millfield Gdns. SE6 8 A1
Millfields Clo. BR5 20 B1
Millwood Rd. BR5 12 C6
Milverston Way. SE9 5 E5
Mimosa Clo. BR6 20 B6
Minden Rd. SE20 6 C4
Ministry Way. SE9 4 D4
Minshull Pl, BR3 7 H3
Minster Rd. BR1 9 F3
Mistletoe Clo. CR0 15 E5
Mitchell Rd. BR6 25 G2
Mitchell Way. BR1 9 E4
Moat Clo. BR6 25 H5
Model Farm Clo. SE9 4 C4
Molash Rd. BR5 20 C1
Molescroft. SE9 5 G5
Monarch Clo. BR4 23 E2
Monivea Rd. BR3 7 G3
Monks Orchard Rd. BR3 15 H5
Monks Way, Monks Orchard. BR3 15 H3
Monks Way, Orpington. BR5 19 E5
Mons Way. BR2 18 A3
Montacute Rd. CR0 22 A6
Montana Gdns. SE26 7 G1
Montbelle Rd. SE9 5 F5
Montbretia Clo. BR5 20 B1
Montcalm Clo. BR2 17 E3
Montrave Rd. SE20 6 D3
Moorcroft Gdns. BR2 18 A2
Mooreland Rd. BR1 9 E3
Moorfield Rd. BR6 20 A4
Morgan Rd. BR1 9 E3
Morgan Wk. BR3 16 A1
Morland Rd, Addiscombe. CR0 14 A5
Morland Rd, Penge. BR3 7 E3
Morley Clo. BR6 18 D6
Morley Rd. BR7 11 E4
Mornington Av. BR1 9 G6
Mornington Clo. TN16 32 D2
Morris Clo, Orpington. BR6 25 F1
Morris Clo, Monks Orchard. CR0 15 E3
Morston Gdns. SE9 4 D6
Mortimer Rd, Leaves Green. TN16 28 D3
Mortimer Rd, Orpington. BR6 20 A5
Moselle Rd. TN16 33 F3
Mosslea Rd, Bromley Common. BR2 17 H2
Mosslea Rd, Farnborough. BR6 24 D1
Mosslea Rd, Penge. SE20 6 D3
Mosul Way. BR2 18 A3
Mosyer Dri. BR5 20 C6
Mottingham Gdns. SE9 4 C3
Mottingham La. SE9 4 A3
Mottingham Rd. SE9 4 C4
Mouchotte Clo. TN16 28 D3
Mount Culver Av. DA14 12 C2
Mount Clo. BR1 10 A4
Mount Court. BR4 16 C6
Mount Pleasant. TN16 32 D2
Mountbatten Gdns. BR3 15 F1
Mountfield Way. BR5 20 B1
Mounthurst Rd. BR2 16 D4
Mountview Rd. BR6 19 H4
Mowbray Rd. SE19 6 A4
Mulberry La. CR0 14 A6
Mungo Park Way. BR5 20 C4
Munnery Way. BR6 18 C6
Murray Av. BR1 9 F5
Murray Rd. BR5 12 B6

Napier Rd, Bromley. BR2 17 F1
Napier Rd, Sth Norwood. SE20 14 C1
Narrow Way. BR2 18 A3
Nash Grn. BR1 9 E2
Nash La. BR2 23 E5
Nelson Clo. TN16 33 E2
Nelson Rd. BR2 17 G1
Netley Clo. CR0 22 B5
Nettlestead Clo. BR3 7 G4
New Barn La. TN14 30 B6
New Farm Av. BR2 17 E1
New Mill Rd. BR5 12 B4
New Rd. BR6 19 H4
New Road Hill. BR6 24 B6
New Street Hill. BR1 9 F1
New Years La. TN14 31 E6
Newbury Rd. BR2 9 E6
Newing Green. BR1 9 H3
Newlands Ct. SE9 5 E1
Newlands Park. SE26 6 D2
Newlyn Clo. BR6 25 H2
Newman Rd. BR1 9 F4
Newnhams Clo. BR1 10 B6
Newports. BR8 21 H4
Newstead Av. BR6 19 F6
Newton Ter. BR2 17 H3
Nichol La. BR1 9 F3
Nicholson Rd. CR0 14 A5
Nicolson Rd. BR5 20 C4
Nightingale Clo. TN16 29 E6
Nightingale La. BR1 9 G5
Nightingale Rd. BR5 18 D3
Ninehams Rd. TN16 32 D6
Ninhams Wood. BR6 24 C2
Norheads La. TN16 32 A4
Norhyrst Av. SE25 6 A6
Norlands Cres. BR7 10 D5
Norlands Gate. BR7 10 D4
Norman Clo. BR6 25 E1
Normanhurst Rd. BR5 12 B5
Norsted La. BR6 31 G2
North Cray Rd. DA14 12 D2
North Dri. BR6 25 G2
North End La. BR6 24 C6
North Pk. SE9 4 D1
North Pole La. BR2 23 E4
North Rd, Bromley. BR1 9 F4
North Rd, West Wickham. BR4 16 A5
North St. BR1 9 E4
North Walk. CR0 22 A4
Northbourne. BR2 17 E4
Northfield Av. BR5 20 B3
Northfield Clo. BR1 10 A4
Northampton Rd. CR0 14 B6
Northlands Av. BR6 25 F2
Northolme Rise. BR6 19 G6
Northside Rd. BR1 9 E4
Northumberland Gdns. BR1 18 B1
Northway Rd. CR0 14 A3
Notson Rd. SE25 14 C2
Novar Clo. BR6 19 H4
Novar Rd. SE9 5 G3
Nugent Rd. SE25 6 A6
Nunnington Clo. SE9 4 C5
Nursery Av. CR0 15 E6
Nursery Clo, Orpington. BR6 19 H4
Nursery Clo, Swanley. BR8 13 H5
Nursery Clo, West Wickham. CR0 14 D6
Nursery Gdns. BR7 10 D2
Nut Tree Clo. BR6 26 D1
Nutfield Way. BR6 18 C6

Oak Av. CR0 15 H5
Oak Gdns. CR0 15 H6
Oak Gro. BR4 16 B6
Oak Lodge Dri. BR4 16 A4
Oak Rd. BR6 25 H5
Oak Tree Gdns. BR1 9 F1
Oak Way. CR0 15 E3
Oakbank. CR0 22 B4
Oakbrook Clo. BR1 9 F1
Oakdene Av. BR7 10 B1
Oakdene Rd. BR5 19 H3
Oakfield Gdns, Eden Park. BR3 15 H2
Oakfield Gdns, Gipsy Hill. SE19 6 A1
Oakfield La. BR2 23 G2
Oakfield Rd, Orpington. BR6 20 A4
Oakfield Rd, Penge. SE20 6 C4
Oakgrove Rd. SE20 6 D5
Oakham Dri. BR2 17 E1
Oakhill Rd, Beckenham. BR3 8 A5
Oakhill Rd, Orpington. BR6 19 G5
Oakhurst Clo. BR7 10 B4
Oaklands Av. BR4 22 A1
Oaklands Clo. BR5 19 F3
Oaklands La. TN16 32 C1
Oaklands Rd. BR1 8 D3
Oakleigh Gdns. BR6 25 G2
Oakleigh Park Av. BR7 10 C4
Oakley Dri, Beckenham. SE9 5 H3
Oakley Dri, Keston Mark. BR2 24 A1
Oakley Rd, Keston Mark. BR2 18 A6
Oakley Rd, Sth Norwood. SE25 14 C2
Oakmead Av. BR2 17 E3
Oakmont Pl. BR6 19 F5
Oakridge Rd. BR1 8 C1
Oakview Gro. CR0 15 F5
Oakview Rd. SE6 7 H1
Oakway. BR2 8 B5
Oakways. SE9 5 F1
Oakwood Av, Beckenham. BR3 8 A5
Oakwood Av, Bromley. BR2 9 F6
Oakwood Clo. BR7 10 B2
Oakwood Gdns. BR6 19 E6
Oakwood Rd. BR6 19 E6
Oasthouse Way. BR5 20 B1
Oates Clo. BR2 8 B6
Oatfield Rd. BR6 19 H5
Ockham Dri. BR5 12 A3
Offenham Rd. SE9 4 D6
Okemore Gdns. BR5 20 B1
Old Bromley Rd. BR1 8 B1
Old Chapel Rd. BR8 21 H4
Old Farm Av. DA15 5 H3
Old Harrow La. TN16 34 A4
Old Hill, Chislehurst. BR7 10 C4
Old Hill, Green Street Green. BR6 25 F4
Old Homesdale Rd. BR2 17 G1
Old La. TN16 33 E6
Old London Rd. TN14 26 D6
Old Maidstone Rd. DA14 13 E3
Old Manor Way. BR7 10 B1
Old Perry St. BR7 11 F3
Old School Clo. BR3 7 E5
Old Tye Av. TN16 33 E1
Oldbury Clo. BR5 20 C1
Oldfield Clo. BR1 18 B1
Oldfield Grange. BR1 18 B1
Oldfield Rd. BR1 18 A1
Oleander Clo. BR6 25 F3
Oliver Av. SE25 14 A1
Oliver Gro. SE25 14 A1
Olyffe Dri. BR3 8 A4
Onslow Cres. BR7 10 D4
Orange Court La. BR6 24 C6
Orchard Av. CR0 15 F4
Orchard Grn. BR6 19 G6
Orchard Gro, Monks Orchard. CR0 15 F4
Orchard Gro, Orpington. BR6 19 H6
Orchard Gro, Penge. SE20 6 B
Orchard Rise. CR0 15 F
Orchard Rd, Bromley. BR1 9 G
Orchard Rd, Farnborough. BR6 24 D
Orchard Rd, Pratts Bottom. BR6 31 G
Orchard Way. CR0 15 F
Oregon Sq. BR6 19 F
Orlestone Gdns. BR6 26 D
Ormonde Av. BR6 18 D
Orpington Rd. BR5 19 G
Orpington-by-Pass. BR6 26 B
Osborne Clo. BR3 15 F
Osgood Av. BR6 25 G
Osgood Gdns. BR6 25 G
Ospringe Clo. SE20 6 D
Osterley Clo. BR5 11 H
Otford Clo, Bickley. BR1 10 C
Otford Clo, Penge. SE20 6 D
Otlinge Rd. BR5 20 D
Ottenden Clo. BR6 25 G
Otters Clo. BR5 20 C
Outram Rd. CR0 14 B
Overbrae. BR3 7 H
Overbury Av. BR3 8 A
Overhill Way. BR3 16 B
Overmead. DA15 5 H
Overstand Clo. BR3 15 H
Overstone Gdns. CR0 15 F
Owen Walk (FP). SE20 6 B
Oxenden Wood Rd. BR6 26 B
Oxford Rd DA14 12 B
Oxhawth Cres. BR2 18 C
Oxlip Clo. CR0 15 E

Packham Clo. BR6 20 B
Paddock Clo. BR6 24 D
Paddock Way. BR7 11 F
Paddocks Clo. BR5 20 C
Padstow Clo. BR6 25 H
Padua Rd. SE20 6 D
Page Heath La. BR1 9 H
Page Heath Villas. BR1 9 H
Pagehurst Rd. CR0 14 B
Paget Gdns. BR7 10 D
Palace Gro, Bromley. BR1 9 F
Palace Gro, Upper Norwood. SE19 6 A
Palace Rd, Bromley. BR1 9 F
Palace Rd, Tatsfield. TN16 33 G
Palace Rd, Upper Norwood. SE19 6 A
Palace Sq. SE19 6 A
Palace View. BR1 9 F
Palewell Clo. BR5 12 A
Pallant Way. BR6 24 C
Palm Av. DA14 12 C
Palmarsh Rd. BR5 20 C
Palmer Ct. BR4 22 B
Palmerston Rd. BR6 25 E
Parish La. BR3 7 E
Parish Mews. BR3 7 E
Park Av, Bromley. BR1 8 D
Park Av, Farnborough. BR6 18 B
Park Av, Orpington. BR6 19 H
Park Av, West Wickham. BR4 16 A
Park End. BR1 8 D
Park Farm Rd. BR1 9 H
Park Gro. BR1 9 F
Park Hill. BR1 18 A
Park Hill Rise. CR0 14 A
Park Hill Rd, Bromley. BR2 8 C
Park Hill Rd, Sidcup. DA15 5 H
Park Mews. BR7 10 D
Park Rd, Beckenham. BR3 7 G
Park Rd, Bromley. BR1 9 F
Park Rd, Chislehurst. BR7 10 D
Park Rd, St Mary Cray. BR5 20 B
Park Rd, Sth Norwood. SE25 14 A
Park Rd, Warlingham. CR6 28 A
Park View. SE12 4 A
Park View Rd. CR0 14 B
Parkfield Way. BR2 18 B
Parkfields. CR0 15 F
Parkgate Rd. BR6 27 G
Parkside Av. BR1 18 A
Parkside Clo. SE20 6 D
Parkview Rd. SE9 5 E
Parkwood. BR3 7 H
Parkwood Rd. TN16 33 F

Street	Ref
St Dunstans Rd. SE25	14 A1
St Francis Clo. BR5	19 G3
St Georges Rd, Beckenham. BR3	7 H4
St Georges Rd, Chislehurst. BR1	10 B5
St Georges Rd, Foots Cray. DA14	12 C2
St Georges Rd, Petts Wood. BR5	19 F3
St Georges Rd West. BR1	10 A5
St Giles Clo. BR6	25 E3
St Hughs Rd. SE20	6 C4
St James's Av. BR3	7 F6
St James Way. DA14	12 D1
St Johns Rd, Penge. SE20	6 D3
St Johns Rd, Petts Wood. BR5	19 F3
St Josephs Clo. BR6	25 G2
St Justin Clo. BR5	12 C6
St Keverne Rd. SE9	4 D6
St Kilda Rd. BR6	19 H5
St Laurence Clo. BR5	12 C6
St Leonards Rise. BR6	25 F2
St Lukes Clo. SE25	14 C3
St Margarets Av. DA15	5 H4
St Margarets Clo. BR6	26 A2
St Marks Clo, Bromley. BR2	9 F6
St Marks Rd, Sth Norwood. SE25	14 B1
St Martins La. BR3	16 A2
St Marys Av. BR2	8 C6
St Marys Clo. BR5	12 B5
St Marys Green. TN16	32 D3
St Marys Gro. TN16	32 D3
St Matthews Dri. BR1	10 B6
St Merryn Ct. BR3	7 G3
St Michaels Clo. BR1	10 A6
St Nicolas La. BR7	10 A4
St Paul's Cray Rd. BR7	11 E4
St Pauls Sq. BR2	9 E5
St Pauls Wood Hill. BR5	11 G5
St Peters Clo. BR7	11 F3
St Peters La. BR5	12 A5
St Thomas Dri. BR5	19 E5
St Timothys Mews. BR1	9 F4
St Winifreds Rd. TN16	33 F3
Salisbury Mews. BR2	18 A2
Salisbury Rd, Sth Norwood. SE25	14 B4
Salisbury Rd, Southborough. BR2	18 A2
Salt Box Hill. TN16	28 C4
Saltwood Clo. BR6	26 B2
Samos Rd. SE20	6 C5
Sanderstead Rd. BR5	20 B3
Sandford Rd. BR2	17 E1
Sandhurst Rd. BR6	25 H2
Sandiland Cres. BR2	16 D6
Sandilands. CR0	14 B6
Sandling Rise. SE9	5 E5
Sandown Rd. SE25	14 C2
Sandpiper Way. BR5	12 C6
Sandpit Rd. BR1	8 C1
Sandringham Rd. BR1	9 E1
Sandway Rd. BR5	20 B1
Sandy La, Orpington. BR6	19 H4
Sandy La, St Paul's Cray. BR5	12 C5
Sandy Ridge. BR7	10 B2
Sandybury. BR6	25 F1
Sangley Rd. SE25	14 A1
Saphora Clo. BR6	25 F3
Sarre Rd. BR5	20 B2
Saville Row. BR2	16 D5
Saxon Rd. BR1	9 E3
Saxville Rd. BR5	12 A6
Sayes Court Rd	20 A1
Scadbury Gdns. BR5	11 H5
Scads Hill Clo. BR6	19 G3
Scarborough Clo. TN16	32 C3
Scarlet Clo. BR5	20 A1
School Rd. BR7	11 E4
Scotney Clo. BR6	24 C2
Scotsdale Clo. BR5	19 G1
Scotts Av. BR2	8 C5
Scotts La. BR2	8 B6
Scotts Rd. BR1	9 E3
Seabrook Dri. BR4	16 C6
Sedgehill Rd. SE6	7 H1
Sedgewood Clo. BR2	16 D4
Sefton Clo. BR5	19 G1
Sefton Rd, Addiscombe. CR0	14 B5
Sefton Rd, Orpington. BR5	19 G1
Selah Dri. BR8	13 H4
Selby Clo. BR7	10 C2
Selby Rd. SE20	6 B5
Selhurst Rd. SE25	14 A1
Sellindge Clo. BR3	7 G3
Selwood Rd. CR0	14 C6
Selwyn Pl. BR5	12 A6
Senlac Rd. SE12	4 A3
Sequoia Gdns. BR6	19 H4
Sermon Dri. BR8	13 H6
Serviden Dri. BR1	9 H4
Seven Acres. BR8	21 H3
Sevenoaks Rd, Green Street Green. BR6	25 G5
Sevenoaks Rd, Orpington. BR6	19 H6
Sevenoaks Rd, Pratts Bottom. BR6	26 A6
Sevenoaks Way. BR5	20 B1
Seward Rd. BR3	7 E5
Seymour Dri. BR2	18 B5
Seymour Pl. SE25	14 C1
Seymour Ter. SE20	6 C4
Seymour Villas. SE20	6 C4
Shaftesbury Rd. BR3	7 G5
Shalford Clo. BR6	25 E2
Shallons Rd. SE9	5 F5
Shannon Way. BR3	7 H2
Sharon Ct. BR1	9 H5
Shaw Rd. TN16	32 D5
Shawfield Park. BR1	9 H5
Shaxton Cres. CR0	22 A6
Sheen Rd. BR5	19 G1
Sheepbarn La. TN16	28 A3
Sheepcote La. BR5	21 E3
Sheldon Clo. SE20	6 C4
Sheldwich Ter. BR2	18 A3
Shelford Rise. SE19	6 A3
Shell Clo. BR2	18 A3
Shelley Clo. BR6	25 G1
Shepherds Clo. BR6	25 G1
Shepherds Grn. BR7	11 F3
Shepperton Rd. BR5	19 E3
Sherborne Rd. BR5	19 G2
Sheridan Cres. BR7	10 D4
Sheridan Way. BR3	7 F4
Sheringham Rd. SE20	6 C6
Sherlies Av. BR6	19 G6
Sherman Rd. BR1	9 E4
Sherwood Rd. BR6	14 C5
Sherwood Way. BR4	16 A6
Shinners Rd. SE25	14 B2
Ship Hill. TN16	32 D6
Shipfield Clo. TN16	32 D6
Shire La. BR6	24 A6
Shirley Av. CR0	14 D5
Shirley Cres. BR3	15 E1
Shirley Oaks Rd. CR0	15 E5
Shirley Pk Rd. CR0	14 C5
Shirley Rd. CR0	14 C4
Shirley Way. CR0	15 G6
Sholden Gdns. BR5	20 B2
Shoreham Clo. CR0	14 D3
Shoreham La. BR6	27 F4
Shoreham Rd, BR5	12 A4
Shoreham Way. BR2	17 E3
Shorne Clo. BR5	20 C1
Shornefield Clo. BR1	10 C6
Shorters Oasts. BR6	31 G1
Shortlands Gdns. BR2	8 D5
Shortlands Gro. BR2	8 C6
Shortlands Rd. BR2	8 B6
Shottery Clo. SE9	4 C5
Shrewsbury Rd. BR3	7 F6
Shrubsall Clo. SE9	4 C3
Shurlock Dri. BR6	24 D2
Sibthorpe Rd. SE12	4 A1
Sidcup By-Pass. BR5	12 A2
Sidcup By-Pass. DA14	5 H4
Sidcup Hill. DA14	12 A1
Sidcup Hill Gdns. DA14	12 B1
Sidcup Rd. SE12	4 A2
Sidewood Rd. SE9	5 H3
Sidmouth Rd. BR5	20 A1
Sidney Rd, Beckenham. BR3	7 F5
Sidney Rd, Sth Norwood. SE25	14 B2
Silver La. BR4	16 B6
Silverdale Dri. SE9	4 C4
Silverdale Rd, Petts Wood. BR5	19 E1
Silverdale Rd, St Paul's Cray. BR5	11 H6
Silverstead La. TN16	34 B6
Silverwood Clo. BR3	7 G3
Simone Clo. BR1	9 H4
Simpsons Rd. BR2	9 E6
Single St. BR6	30 A6
Singles Cross La. TN14	31 G5
Siward Rd. BR2	9 F6
Skeet Hill La. BR6	20 D5
Skibbs La. BR5	21 E6
Skid Hill La. CR6	32 A1
Skyneley Rd. SE12	4 B5
Slades Dri. BR7	5 G5
Sloane Gdns. BR6	25 E1
Sloane Wk. CR0	15 F3
Smarden Gro. SE9	4 D5
Snag La. TN14	30 C3
Snodland Clo. BR6	29 H1
Snowdown Clo. SE20	6 D4
Socket La. BR2	17 F4
Somerden Rd. BR5	20 C4
Somerset Rd. BR6	19 H4
Somerville Rd. SE20	7 E3
Sonnet Walk. TN16	32 C3
Sonning Rd. SE25	14 B4
Sopwith Clo. TN16	32 D1
Sounds Lodge. BR8	21 H3
South App. SE9	4 D3
South Bank. BR7	5 G5
South Dri. BR6	25 F3
South Eden Park Rd. BR3	16 A1
South Hill. BR7	10 B3
South Hill Rd. BR2	16 C1
South Norwood Hill. SE25	6 A5
South St. BR1	9 E5
South Walk. BR4	22 C1
South Way. BR2	17 E4
Southborough La. BR2	18 A2
Southborough Rd. BR1	18 A2
Southbourne. BR2	17 E4
Southcote Rd. SE25	14 C3
Southcroft Av. BR4	16 A6
Southcroft Rd. BR6	25 G1
Southend Clo. SE9	5 F1
Southend Cres. SE9	5 F1
Southend Rd. BR3	7 H4
Southern Av. SE25	6 A6
Southey St. SE20	6 D3
Southfield Rd. BR5	11 H6
Southfleet Rd. BR6	25 G2
Southill Rd. BR7	10 A3
Southlands Av. BR6	25 F3
Southlands Gro. BR1	10 A6
Southlands Rd. BR1	18 A1
Southold Rise. SE9	5 E5
Southover. BR1	9 E2
Southspring. DA15	5 H2
Southview. BR1	9 G5
Southwark Pl. BR1	18 B1
Southwater Clo. BR3	8 A3
Southwood Clo. BR1	18 B1
Southwood Rise. SE9	5 E5
Southwood Rd. SE9	5 F4
Sparrow Dri. BR5	19 E5
Sparrows La. SE9	5 G2
Spekehill. SE9	4 D5
Speldhurst Clo. BR2	17 E2
Spencer Clo. BR6	19 G6
Spencer Rd. BR1	8 D3
Spinney Clo. BR3	16 A1
Spinney Gdns. SE19	6 A1
Spinney Oak. BR1	10 A5
Spinney Way. TN14	30 C2
Spring Gdns, Biggin Hill. TN16	32 C3
Spring Gdns, Chelsfield. BR6	26 A4
Spring Gro. SE20	6 A3
Spring La. SE25	14 C3
Spring Park Av. CR0	15 E6
Spring Park Rd. CR0	15 E6
Spring Shaw Rd. BR5	11 H4
Springbourne Ct. BR3	8 B4
Springfield Gdns, Southborough. BR1	18 B1
Springfield Gdns, West Wickham. BR4	16 A6
Springfield Rd, Penge. SE26	6 C2
Springfield Rd, Southborough. BR1	18 B1
Springholm Clo. TN16	32 D3
Springpark Dri. BR3	8 B6
Springvale Way. BR5	12 B6
Spruce Rd. TN16	33 E3
Spur Rd. BR6	20 A6
Squires Wood Dri. BR7	10 A3
Squirrel Clo. BR6	19 F5
Stables End. BR6	25 E1
Stainmore Clo. BR7	11 F4
Stalisfield Pl. BR6	29 H1
Stambourne Way, Upper Norwood. SE19	6 A4
Stambourne Way, West Wickham. BR4	22 B1
Stamford Dri. BR2	16 D1
Standard Rd. BR6	29 H1
Stanger Rd. SE25	14 B3
Stanhope Av. BR2	17 E6
Stanhope Gro. BR3	15 G2
Stanley Av. BR3	8 B6
Stanley Rd, Bromley. BR2	17 G1
Stanley Rd, Orpington. BR6	19 H5
Stanley Way. BR5	20 A2
Stanmore Ter. BR3	7 H5
Stanstead Clo. BR2	17 E3
Stanton Clo. BR5	20 B4
Stapleton Rd. BR6	25 G1
Star La. BR5	20 B1
Starts Clo. BR6	24 C1
Starts Hill Av. BR6	24 D3
Starts Hill Rd. BR6	24 C1
State Farm Av. BR6	24 D2
Station Approach, Chelsfield. BR6	26 A3
Station Approach, Chislehurst. BR7	10 C4
Station Approach, Elmstead Woods. BR7	10 A2
Station Approach, Hayes. BR2	17 E5
Station Approach, Orpington. BR6	19 G6
Station Approach, St Mary Cray. BR5	20 A1
Station Approach, Sydenham. SE26	7 G1
Station Hill. BR2	17 E6
Station Rd, Bromley. BR1	9 E4
Station Rd, Orpington. BR6	19 G6
Station Rd, Penge. SE20	6 D2
Station Rd, St Mary Cray. BR5	20 B1
Station Rd, Shortlands. BR2	8 D5
Station Rd, Sth Norwood. SE25	14 A1
Station Rd, West Wickham. BR4	16 B5
Station Sq. BR5	19 E2
Steep Clo. BR6	25 H4
Steeple Heights Dri. TN16	32 D2
Stembridge Rd. SE20	6 C5
Stephen Clo. BR6	25 G1
Steve Biko La. SE6	7 H1
Stevens Clo. BR3	7 H2
Stewart Clo. BR7	5 F6
Steyning Gro. SE9	4 D6
Stiles Clo. BR2	18 B3
Stirling Dri. BR6	26 A3
Stock Hill. TN16	32 D2
Stockbury Rd. CR0	14 D3
Stockwell Clo. BR1	9 F5
Stodart Rd. SE20	6 D4
Stofield Gdns. SE9	4 B5
Stokes Rd. CR0	15 E3
Stone Park Av. BR3	15 H1
Stone Rd. BR2	17 E2
Stonegate Clo. BR5	12 B6
Stonehill Green Rd. DA2	13 H3
Stonehouse La. TN14	26 C6
Stonehouse Rd. TN14	26 C6
Stoneings La. TN14	34 D4
Stoneleigh Pk Av. CR0	15 E3
Stones Cross Rd. BR8	21 H2

Stoney La. SE19 — 6 A2
Storrington Rd. CR0 — 14 A5
Stour Clo. BR4 — 23 G2
Stowe Rd. BR6 — 26 B2
Stowting Rd. BR6 — 25 G2
Stratford Ho Av. BR1 — 10 A6
Strathaven Rd. SE12 — 4 A1
Streamside Clo. BR2 — 17 E1
Stretton Rd. CR0 — 14 A4
Strickland Way. BR6 — 25 G2
Stroud Green Gdns. CR0 — 14 C4
Stroud Green Way. CR0 — 14 C4
Stroud Rd. SE25 — 14 B3
Stuart Av. BR2 — 17 E5
Stubbs Hill. TN14 — 31 G5
Studland Rd. SE26 — 7 E2
Studley Ct. DA14 — 12 B1
Stumps Hill La. BR3 — 7 H2
Sturges Field. BR7 — 11 F3
Styles Rd. BR3 — 16 B1
Sudbury Cres. BR1 — 9 E2
Suffield Rd. SE20 — 6 C5
Suffolk Rd,
  Foots Cray. DA14 — 12 B2
Suffolk Rd,
  Sth Norwood. SE25 — 14 A1
Sultan St. BR3 — 7 E5
Summer Hill. BR1 — 10 C5
Summerhill Clo. BR6 — 25 F2
Summerhill Villas. BR7 — 10 C4
Summit Way. SE19 — 6 A3
Sumner Clo. BR6 — 24 D2
Sundial Av. SE25 — 6 A6
Sundridge Av. BR1 — 9 H4
Sundridge Rd. CR0 — 14 A5
Sunningdale Rd. BR1 — 18 A1
Sunningvale Av. TN16 — 32 D1
Sunningvale Clo. TN16 — 32 D1
Sunny Bank. SE25 — 6 B6
Sunny Croft Rd. SE25 — 14 B1
Sunnydale. BR6 — 18 C6
Sunnyfield Rd. BR5 — 11 H6
Sunray Av. BR2 — 18 A3
Sunset Gdns. SE25 — 6 A5
Superior Dri. BR6 — 25 G4
Surrey Rd. BR4 — 16 A5
Susan Wood. BR7 — 10 C4
Sussex Rd,
  Foots Cray. DA14 — 12 B1
Sussex Rd,
  St Mary Cray. BR5 — 20 B3
Sussex Rd,
  West Wickham. BR4 — 16 A5
Sutherland Av,
  Biggin Hill. TN16 — 33 E2
Sutherland Av,
  Petts Wood. BR5 — 19 G3
Sutton Clo. BR3 — 8 A4
Suttons Gdns. CR0 — 14 A2
Swallowtail Clo. BR5 — 20 C1
Swan Clo. BR1 — 12 A6
Swanley By-Pass. BR8 — 21 H1
Sward Rd. BR5 — 19 H3
Sweeps La. BR5 — 20 C2
Swievelands Way. TN16 — 32 C4
Swifsden Way. BR1 — 8 D2
Swinburne Cres. CR0 — 14 D4
Swires Shaw. BR2 — 23 H2
Swithland Gdns. SE9 — r5 E6
Sycamore Clo. SE9 — 4 C4
Sycamore Gro. SE20 — 6 B4
Sydenham Av. SE26 — 6 C1
Sydenham Rd. SE26 — 6 D1
Sylvan Hill. SE19 — 6 A4
Sylvan Rd. SE19 — 6 A4
Sylvan Walk. BR1 — 10 B6
Sylvan Way. BR4 — 22 C2
Sylvester Av. BR7 — 10 B2

Tall Elms Clo. BR2 — 16 D2
Tandridge Pl. BR6 — 19 F5
Tandridge Rd. BR6 — 19 F5
Tangleberry Clo. BR2 — 18 A6
Tannery Clo. BR3 — 15 E2
Tansfield Rd. SE26 — 7 E1
Tarnwood Park. SE9 — 4 D2
Tarragon Gro. SE26 — 6 D2
Tatsfield La. TN16 — 33 F6
Tatsfield Rd. TN16 — 32 C6
Tavistock Rd. BR2 — 17 E1
Taylor Clo. BR6 — 25 G2

Teal Av. BR5 — 20 C1
Teasle Clo. CR0 — 14 D5
Teevan Clo. CR0 — 14 B4
Teevan Rd. CR0 — 14 B4
Telford Clo. SE19 — 6 A2
Telford Rd. SE9 — 5 G4
Telscombe Clo. BR6 — 19 G6
Temple Av. CR0 — 15 F6
Temple Rd. TN16 — 33 E2
Tennison Rd. SE25 — 14 A1
Tennyson Rd. SE20 — 7 E3
Tent Peg La. BR5 — 18 D2
Tenterden Clo. SE9 — 4 D6
Tenterden Gdns. CR0 — 14 B4
Tenterden Rd. CR0 — 14 B4
Tetty Way. BR2 — 9 E5
Teynham Grn. BR2 — 17 E2
Thackeram Clo. SE26 — 6 C1
Thanet Dri. BR2 — 23 H2
Thaxted Rd. SE9 — 5 G4
Thayers Farm Rd. BR3 — 7 F4
The Alders. BR4 — 15 H5
The Approach. BR6 — 19 H6
The Avenue,
  Beckenham. BR3 — 8 A4
The Avenue, Bromley. BR1 — 9 H6
The Avenue, Keston. BR4 — 23 H2
The Avenue, Orpington. BR6 — 19 H6
The Avenue,
  St Paul's Cray. BR5 — 12 A3
The Avenue,
  West Wickham. BR4 — 16 B4
The Birches. BR6 — 24 C2
The Brackens. BR6 — 25 H3
The Chase. BR1 — 9 F6
The Chenies. BR6 — 19 G3
The Chummery. BR2 — 16 C5
The Close, Elmers End. BR3 — 15 F1
The Close, Foots Cray. DA14 — 12 B1
The Close, Petts Wood. BR5 — 19 F3
The Coppins. CR0 — 22 A4
The Course. SE9 — 5 E5
The Covert. BR6 — 19 F3
The Crescent,
  Beckenham. BR3 — 7 H4
The Crescent,
  Park Langley. BR4 — 16 C3
The Croft. BR8 — 13 H6
The Crossway. SE9 — 4 C4
The Dale. BR2 — 23 H2
The Dell. SE19 — 6 A4
The Drift. BR2 — 23 H1
The Drive, Beckenham. BR3 — 7 G5
The Drive, Orpington. BR6 — 19 H6
The Drive,
  St Paul's Cray. BR5 — 11 G6
The Drive,
  West Wickham. BR4 — 16 B4
The Fairway. BR1 — 18 B2
The Gardens. BR3 — 8 B5
The Glade, Bromley. BR1 — 9 H5
The Glade,
  Monks Orchard. CR0 — 15 E2
The Glade,
  West Wickham. BR4 — 22 A1
The Glebe. BR7 — 11 E4
The Glen, Bromley. BR2 — 8 C5
The Glen, Farnborough. BR6 — 18 C6
The Grange. BR6 — 15 G6
The Green, Crockenhill. BR8 — 21 H3
The Green, Hayes. BR2 — 17 E4
The Green,
  St Paul's Cray. BR5 — 12 A3
The Green, Sidcup. DA14 — 11 H1
The Greenway. BR5 — 20 A3
The Grove, Biggin Hill. TN16 — 33 E3
The Grove, Foots Cray. DA14 — 12 D1
The Grove,
  West Wickham. BR4 — 16 A6
The Heights. BR3 — 8 B3
The Highway. BR2 — 26 B3
The Hillside. BR6 — 26 A6
The Knole. SE9 — 5 E6
The Knoll, Beckenham. BR3 — 8 A4
The Knoll, Hayes. BR2 — 17 E5
The Landway. BR5 — 12 B6
The Laurels. BR2 — 17 E1
The Lees. CR0 — 15 G6
The Limes. BR2 — 18 A6
The Lindens. CR0 — 22 A4
The Mall. BR1 — 9 E6

The Maltings. BR6 — 19 G5
The Mead, Beckenham. BR3 — 8 A5
The Mead,
  West Wickham. BR4 — 16 B5
The Meadow. BR7 — 11 E2
The Meadows. BR6 — 26 B4
The Meadway. BR6 — 26 A3
The Mound. SE9 — 5 E5
The Nower. TN14 — 34 D4
The Old Courtyard. BR1 — 9 F4
The Pantiles. BR1 — 10 A6
The Park, Sidcup. DA14 — 11 H1
The Park,
  Upper Norwood. SE19 — 6 A3
The Rosery. CR0 — 14 D3
The Spinney. DA14 — 12 D1
The Square. TN16 — 32 D6
The Squirrels. BR2 — 18 A5
The Retreat. BR6 — 26 A4
The Ridge. BR6 — 19 F6
The Ridings. TN16 — 33 E2
The Spinneys. BR1 — 10 B5
The Underdown. SE9 — 5 E4
The Vale. CR0 — 15 E6
The Vista. SE9 — 4 B1
The Weald. BR7 — 10 B2
The Woodlands,
  Beckenham. BR3 — 8 A4
The Woodlands,
  Chelsfield. BR6 — 26 B4
Thesiger Rd. SE20 — 7 E3
Thicket Gro. SE20 — 6 B3
Thicket Rd. SE20 — 6 B3
Thirlmere Rise. BR1 — 8 D2
Thistlemead. BR7 — 10 C5
Thomas Dinwiddy Rd. SE12 — 4 A4
Thorn Clo. BR2 — 18 C3
Thorndon Clo. BR5 — 11 H4
Thorndon Rd. BR5 — 11 H5
Thornes Clo. BR3 — 8 A6
Thornet Wood Rd. BR1 — 10 C6
Thornsett Pl. SE20 — 6 C5
Thornsett Rd. SE20 — 6 C5
Thornton Dene. BR3 — 7 G5
Thornton Rd. BR1 — 9 E1
Thorpe Clo. BR6 — 19 G6
Thrift La. TN14 — 34 C3
Thurbarn Rd. SE6 — 7 H1
Thursland Rd. DA14 — 12 D2
Thursley Cres. CR0 — 22 B5
Thursley Rd. SE9 — 4 D5
Thyer Clo. BR6 — 24 D2
Tiepigs La. BR4 — 16 D6
Tiger Av. BR2 — 17 F1
Tilbury Clo. BR5 — 12 B5
Tile Farm Rd. BR6 — 25 F1
Tillingbourne Grn. BR5 — 19 H1
Tiltyard App. SE9 — 4 D1
Timber Clo. BR7 — 10 C4
Timber Top Rd. TN16 — 32 D3
Tintagel Rd. BR5 — 20 B6
Tiverton Dri. SE9 — 5 G3
Tonge Clo. BR3 — 15 H2
Tootswood Rd. BR2 — 16 C2
Top Park. BR3 — 16 C2
Torr Rd. SE20 — 7 E3
Torver Way. BR6 — 19 E6
Tovil Clo. SE20 — 6 B5
Tower Clo, Orpington. BR6 — 25 H1
Tower Clo, Penge. SE20 — 6 C3
Tower Rd. BR6 — 19 G6
Tower Rd. SE20 — 15 E4
Towncourt Cres. BR5 — 19 E2
Towncourt La. BR5 — 19 E3
Townsend Clo. DA14 — 12 B2
Townshend Rd. BR7 — 10 D1
Toynbec Clo. BR7 — 5 F6
Transmere Rd. BR5 — 19 E3
Transmere Rd. BR5 — 19 E3
Tredwell Rd. BR1 — 18 A1
Treebourne Rd. TN16 — 32 D3
Treewall Gdns. BR1 — 9 F1
Tregony Rd. BR6 — 25 H2
Tremaine Rd. SE20 — 6 C5
Trenear Clo. BR6 — 25 H2
Trenholme Clo. SE20 — 6 C3
Trenholme Rd. SE20 — 6 C3
Trenholme Ter. SE20 — 6 C3
Trentham Dri. BR5 — 20 A2

Tresco Clo. BR1 — 8 C2
Trevor Clo. BR2 — 17 E4
Trewsbury Rd. SE26 — 7 E1
Trinity Clo. BR2 — 18 A5
Trinity Mews. SE20 — 6 C5
Trunks Alley. BR8 — 13 G5
Tubbenden Clo. BR6 — 25 F1
Tubbenden Dri. BR6 — 25 F2
Tubbenden La. BR6 — 25 F2
Tubbenden Lane Sth. BR6 — 25 E3
Tudor Clo. BR7 — 10 B4
Tudor Ct. BR8 — 21 H4
Tudor Gdns. BR4 — 22 A1
Tudor Rd, Beckenham. BR3 — 8 A6
Tudor Rd,
  Sth Norwood. SE25 — 14 C3
Tudor Rd,
  Upper Norwood. SE19 — 6 A3
Tudor Way. BR5 — 19 E3
Tugmutton Clo. BR6 — 24 D2
Tulip Clo. CR0 — 14 D5
Tulse Clo. BR3 — 8 A6
Tunstall Clo. BR6 — 25 G2
Tunstall Rd. CR0 — 14 A5
Turnberry Way. BR6 — 19 F5
Turner Rd. TN16 — 28 D4
Turners Meadow Way. BR3 — 7 F4
Turnpike Dri. BR6 — 26 C6
Turpington Clo. BR2 — 18 A4
Turpington La. BR2 — 18 A4
Tweedy Rd. BR1 — 9 E4
Tye La. BR6 — 25 E3
Tylers Grn Rd. BR8 — 21 H3
Tylney Av. SE19 — 6 A1
Tylney Rd. BR1 — 9 H5
Tyron Way. DA14 — 11 G1

Ullswater Clo. BR1 — 8 D3
Underwood. CR0 — 22 A3
Union Rd. BR2 — 17 H2
Unity Clo. CR0 — 22 A6
Upchurch Clo. SE20 — 6 C3
Upfield. CR0 — 14 C6
Uplands. BR3 — 7 G6
Uplands Rd. BR6 — 20 A5
Upper Dri. TN16 — 32 D3
Upper Elmers End Rd. BR3 — 15 F1
Upper Grove. SE25 — 14 A1
Upper Park Rd. BR1 — 9 F4
Upper Shirley Rd. CR0 — 14 D6
Upperton Rd. DA14 — 11 H1
Upton Ct. SE20 — 6 D3

Valan Leas. BR2 — 8 D6
Vale Clo. BR6 — 24 C2
Vale Rd. BR1 — 10 B5
Valentyne Clo. CR0 — 28 A2
Valeswood Rd. BR1 — 8 D2
Valley Rd,
  Bromley. BR2 — 8 C5
Valley Rd,
  St Paul's Cray. BR5 — 12 A4
Valley View. TN16 — 32 D3
Valley Wk. CR0 — 14 D6
Valliers Wood Rd. DA15 — 5 H3
Vanburgh Clo. BR6 — 19 F5
Vancouver Clo. BR6 — 25 H2
Venner Rd. SE26 — 6 D2
Verdayne Av. CR0 — 15 E6
Vernon Clo. BR5 — 12 B6
Versailles Rd. SE20 — 6 B3
Veryan Clo. BR5 — 20 B1
Vicarage Dri. BR3 — 7 G4
Victor Rd. SE20 — 7 E3
Victory Pl. SE19 — 6 A3
Victoria Gdns. TN16 — 28 D6
Victoria Rd, Chislehurst. BR7 — 10 C1
Victoria Rd,
  Southborough. BR2 — 18 A2
View Clo. TN16 — 32 C2
Viewlands Av. TN16 — 34 D5
Village Green Av. TN16 — 33 F2
Village Green Way. TN16 — 33 E3
Village Way. BR3 — 7 G6
Villiers Rd. BR3 — 7 E5
Vincent Clo, Bromley. BR2 — 17 F1
Vincent Clo, Sidcup. DA15 — 5 H3
Vincent Sq. TN16 — 28 D4
Vine Rd. BR6 — 25 H4
Vinson Clo. BR6 — 19 H5